KB052946

THE TIGER RISING

Kate DiCamillo

THE TIGER RISING
Copyright © 2001 by Kate DiCamillo

ISBN 979-11-91343-87-8 14740

Longtail Books
3rd Floor, 113, Yanghwa-ro, Mapo-gu, Seoul

I am grateful to Matt Pogatshnik

for giving me the music,

Bill Mockler for always reading,

the McKnight Foundation

for bestowing peace of mind,

Jane Resh Thomas for shining a light

on the path, Tracey Bailey

and Lisa Beck for being my

"death of the hired man" friends,

my mother for telling me not

to give up, and to Kara LaReau

for believing that I could . . .

and that I can. And that I will.

chapter

1

That morning, after he discovered the tiger, Rob went and
stood under the Kentucky Star Motel sign and waited for
the school bus just like it was any other day. The Kentucky
Star sign was **compose**d of a yellow neon★ star that rose
and fell over a piece of blue neon in the shape of the state
of Kentucky. Rob liked the sign; he **harbor**ed a **dim** but
abiding notion that it would bring him good luck.

Finding the tiger had been luck, he knew that. He had
been out in the woods behind the Kentucky Star Motel,
way out in the woods, not really looking for anything, just
wandering, hoping that maybe he would get lost or get
eaten by a bear and not have to go to school ever again.
That's when he saw the old Beauchamp gas station✻

★ neon 네온사인. 방전관 내부에 주입하는 가스에 따라 여러가지 색을 낸다.
✻ gas station 주유소.

building, all **board**ed up and **tumbling** down; next to it, there was a cage, and inside the cage, unbelievably, there was a tiger—a real-life, very large tiger **pacing** back and forth. He was orange and gold and so bright, it was like **staring** at the sun itself, angry and **trap**ped in a cage.

It was early morning and it looked like it might rain; it had been raining every day for almost two weeks. The sky was gray and the air was thick and **still**. Fog was hugging the ground. To Rob, it seemed as if the tiger was some magic **trick**, rising out of the **mist**. He was so **astound**ed at his discovery, so **amaze**d, that he stood and stared. But only for a minute; he was afraid to look at the tiger for too long, afraid that the tiger would disappear. He stared, and then he turned and ran back into the woods, toward the Kentucky Star. And the whole way home, while his brain **doubt**ed what he had seen, his heart **beat** out the truth to him. *Ti-ger. Ti-ger. Ti-ger.*

That was what Rob thought about as he stood **beneath** the Kentucky Star sign and waited for the bus. The tiger. He did not think about the **rash** on his legs, the **itchy** red **blister**s that **snake**d their way into his shoes. His father said that it would be less likely to itch if he didn't think about it.

And he did not think about his mother. He hadn't thought about her since the morning of the **funeral**, the morning he couldn't stop crying the great **heaving sob**s that made his chest and stomach hurt. His father, watching him, standing beside him, had started to cry, too.

They were both dressed up in suits that day; his father's suit was too small. And when he **slap**ped Rob to make him stop crying, he **rip**ped a hole underneath the arm of his jacket.

"There ain't* no point in crying," his father had said **afterward**. "Crying ain't going to bring her back."

It had been six months since that day, six months since he and his father had moved from Jacksonville to Lister, and Rob had not cried since, not once.

The final thing he did not think about that morning was getting onto the bus. He **specific**ally did not think about Norton and Billy Threemonger waiting for him like **chain**ed and **starved guard** dogs, **eager** to attack.

Rob had a way of not-thinking about things. He imagined himself as a **suitcase** that was too full, like the one that he had packed when they left Jacksonville after the funeral. He made all his feelings go inside the suitcase; he **stuff**ed them in tight and then sat on the suitcase and locked it shut. That was the way he not-thought about things. Sometimes it was hard to keep the suitcase shut.

★ ain't am[are, is] not의 단축형, 구어체.

But now he had something to put on top of it. The tiger.

So as he waited for the bus under the Kentucky Star sign, and as the first drops of rain fell from the **sullen** sky, Rob imagined the tiger on top of his suitcase, **blink**ing his golden eyes, sitting proud and strong, **unaffected** by all the not-thoughts inside **strain**ing to come out.

2

"Looky* here," said Norton Threemonger as soon as Rob stepped onto the school bus. "It's the Kentucky Star. How's it feel to be a star?" Norton stood in the center of the **aisle, block**ing Rob's path.

Rob **shrugged.**

"Oh, he don't know," Norton called to his brother. "Hey, Billy, he don't know what it's like to be a star."

Rob **slipp**ed past Norton. He walked all the way to the back of the bus and sat down in the last seat.

"Hey," said Billy Threemonger, "you know what? This ain't Kentucky. This is Florida."

He followed Rob and sat down right next to him. He pushed his face so close that Rob could smell his breath. It

---

*looky 'look at'의 구어체. 자, 봐!

was bad breath. It smelled **metallic** and **rot**ten. "You ain't a Kentucky star," Billy said, his eyes **glow**ing under the **brim** of his John Deere* cap. "And you sure ain't a star here in Florida. You ain't a star nowhere."

"Okay," said Rob.

Billy **shoved** him hard. And then Norton came **swagger**ing back and **lean**ed over Billy and **grab**bed hold of Rob's hair with one hand, and with the other hand **ground** his **knuckle**s into Rob's **scalp**.

Rob sat there and took it. If he fought back, it lasted longer. If he didn't fight back, sometimes they got **bored** and left him alone. They were the only three kids on the bus until it got into town and Mr. Nelson, the driver, **pretend**ed like he didn't know what was going on. He drove **staring** straight ahead, **whistling** songs that didn't have any melody. Rob was **on his own**, and he knew it.

"He's got the **creep**ing **crud** all over him," said Billy. He pointed at Rob's legs. "Look," he said to Norton. "Ain't it **gross?**"

"Uh-huh," said Norton. He was **concentrating** on grinding his knuckles into Rob's head. It hurt, but Rob didn't cry. He never cried. He was a pro at not-crying. He

---

*John Deere 미국을 대표하는 농기구 제작 업체. 정식 이름은 Deere & Company이지만, John Deere라는 애칭으로 더 많이 불린다. 사슴로고가 새겨진 티셔츠와 야구 모자가 유명하다.

was the best not-crier in the world. It **drove** Norton and Billy Threemonger wild. And today Rob had the extra power of the tiger. All he had to do was think about it, and he knew there was no way he would cry. Not ever.

They were still out in the country, only halfway into town, when the bus **lurch**ed to a stop. This was such a surprising development, to have the bus stop halfway through its **route**, that Norton stopped grinding his knuckles into Rob's scalp and Billy stopped **punch**ing Rob in the arm.

"Hey, Mr. Nelson," Norton shouted. "Whatcha doin'?★"

"This ain't a stop, Mr. Nelson," Billy called out helpfully.

But Mr. Nelson **ignore**d them. He kept whistling his non-song as he **swung** open the bus door. And while Norton and Billy and Rob watched, **open-mouthed** and silent, a girl with yellow hair and a pink **lacy** dress walked up the steps and onto the bus.

★ whatcha doin' 'what are you doing'의 구어체.

chapter

3

Nobody wore pink **lacy** dresses to school. Nobody. Even
Rob knew that. He held his breath as he watched the girl
walk down the **aisle** of the bus. Here was somebody even
stranger than he was. He was sure.

"Hey," Norton called, "this is a school bus."

"I know it," the girl said. Her voice was **gravelly** and
deep, and the words sounded **clipped** and strange, like she
was **stamp**ing each one of them out with a cookie cutter.★

"You're all dressed up to go to a party," Billy said. "This
ain't the party bus." He **elbow**ed Rob in the **ribs**.

"Haw." Norton laughed. He gave Rob a friendly **thud**
on the head.

The girl stood in the center of the aisle, **sway**ing with

★ cookie cutter 쿠키를 찍는 틀.

the movement of the bus. She **stared** at them. "It's not my **fault** you don't have good clothes," she said finally. She sat down and put her back to them.

"Hey," said Norton. "We're sorry. We didn't mean nothing. Hey," he said again. "What's your name?"

The girl turned and looked at them. She had a sharp nose and a sharp **chin** and black, black eyes.

"Sistine," she said.

"Sistine," **hoot**ed Billy. "What kind of stupid name is that?"

"Like the **chapel**," she said slowly, making each word clear and strong.

Rob stared at her, **amaze**d.

"What are you looking at?" she said to him.

Rob shook his head.

"Yeah," said Norton. He **cuff**ed Rob on the ear. "What are you staring at, **disease** boy? Come on," he said to Billy.

And together they **swagger**ed up the aisle of the bus and sat in the seat behind the new girl.

They **whisper**ed things to her, but Rob couldn't hear what they were saying. He thought about the Sistine Chapel.★ He had seen a picture of it in the big art book that Mrs.

★Sistine Chapel 시스티나 성당. 바티칸 시국에 있는 교황의 개인적인 성당이자 새로운 교황을 선출하기 위해 추기경단이 비밀회의를 여는 장소이다. 미켈란젤로가 그린 전설적인 프레스코화가 천장에 그려져 있다.

Dupree kept on a small shelf behind her desk in the library. The pages of the book were **slick** and shiny. And each picture made Rob feel cool and sweet inside, like a drink of water on a hot day. Mrs. Dupree let Rob look at the book because he was quiet and good in the library. It was her **reward** to him.

In the book, the picture from the **ceiling** of the Sistine Chapel★ showed God reaching out and touching Adam. It was like they were playing a game of tag,✳ like God was making Adam "it.✳" It was a beautiful picture.

Rob looked out the window at the gray rain and the gray sky and the gray **highway**. He thought about the tiger. He thought about God and Adam. And he thought about Sistine. He did not think about the **rash**. He did not think about his mother. And he did not think about Norton and Billy Threemonger. He kept the **suitcase** closed.

14

chapter

4

Sistine was in Rob's sixth-grade homeroom class.★ Mrs.
Soames made her stand up and introduce herself.

"My name," she said in her **gravelly** voice, "is Sistine
Bailey." She stood at the front of the room, in her pink
dress. And all the kids stared at her with open mouths as
if she had just stepped off a spaceship from another **planet**.
Rob looked down at his desk. He knew not to stare at her.
He started working on a drawing of the tiger.

"What a lovely name," said Mrs. Soames.

"Thank you," said Sistine.

Patrice Wilkins, who sat in front of Rob, **snort**ed and
then **giggle**d and then covered her mouth.

"I'm from Philadelphia, Pennsylvania," Sistine said,

★ homeroom class 담임 선생님과 매일 정해진 시간에 학교 생활에 대한 사항을 나누는 학
급 조회 시간.

"home of the Liberty Bell,* and I hate the South because the people in it are **ignorant**. And I'm not staying here in Lister. My father is coming to get me next week." She looked around the room **defiant**ly.

"Well," said Mrs. Soames, "thank you very much for introducing yourself, Sistine Bailey. You may take your seat before you **put your foot in your mouth** any **farther**."

The whole class laughed at that. Rob looked up just as Sistine sat down. She **glare**d at him. Then she **stuck** her tongue out at him. *Him!* He shook his head and went back to his drawing.

He sketched out the tiger, but what he wanted to do was **whittle** it in wood. His mother had shown him how to whittle, how to take a piece of wood and make it come alive. She taught him when she was sick. He sat on the **edge** of the bed and watched her tiny white hands closely.

"Don't **jiggle** that bed," his father said. "Your mama's in a lot of pain."

"He ain't hurting me, Robert," his mother said.

"Don't get all tired out with that wood," his father said.

"It's all right," his mother said. "I'm just teaching Rob some things I know."

But she said she didn't have to teach him much. His

★ Liberty Bell 자유의 종. 1776년 7월 4일 미국의 독립을 알린 종으로 필라델피아에 있다.

mother told him he already knew what to do. His hands knew; that's what she said.

"Rob," said the teacher, "I need you to go to the **principal**'s office."

Rob didn't hear her. He was working on the tiger, trying to remember what his eyes looked like.

"Robert," Mrs. Soames said. "Robert Horton." Rob looked up. Robert was his father's name. Robert was what his mother had called his father. "Mr. Phelmer wants to see you in his office. Do you understand?"

"Yes, ma'am," said Rob.

He got up and took his picture of the tiger and folded it up and put it in the back pocket of his shorts. On his way out of the classroom, Jason Uttmeir **tripp**ed him and said, "See you later, retard,*" and Sistine looked up at him with her tiny black eyes. She shot him a look of pure hate.

★ retard 모자라는 사람. 저능아.

5

The **principal**'s office was small and dark and smelled like pipe tobacco.* The **secretary** looked up at Rob when he walked in. "Go right on back," she said, **nod**ding her big blond head of hair. "He's waiting for you."

"Rob," said Mr. Phelmer when Rob stepped into his office.

"Yes, sir," said Rob.

"Have a seat," Mr. Phelmer said, **waving** his hand at the orange plastic chair in front of his desk.

Rob sat down.

Mr. Phelmer cleared his **throat**. He **pat**ted the piece of hair that was **comb**ed over his **bald** head. He cleared his throat again. "Rob, we're a bit worried," he finally said.

★ pipe tobacco 파이프 담배.

Rob nodded. This was how Mr. Phelmer began all his talks with Rob. He was always worried: worried that Rob did not **interact** with the other students, worried that he did not communicate, worried that he wasn't doing well, in any way, at school.

"It's about your, uh, legs. Yes. Your legs. Have you been putting that medicine on them?"

"Yes, sir," said Rob. He didn't look at Mr. Phelmer. He stared instead at the **panel**ed wall behind the principal's head. It was covered with an **astonish**ing **array** of **framed** pieces of paper—**certificate**s and **diploma**s and thank-you letters.

"May I, uh, look?" asked Mr. Phelmer. He got up from his chair and came halfway around his desk and stared at Rob's legs.

"Well, sir," he said after a minute. He went back behind his desk and sat down. He folded his hands together and **crack**ed his **knuckles**. He cleared his throat.

"Here's the situation, Rob. Some of the parents— I won't mention any names—are worried that what you've got there might be **contagious**, *contagious* meaning something that the other students could possibly catch." Mr. Phelmer cleared his throat again. He stared at Rob.

"Tell me the truth, son," he said. "Have you been using that medicine you told me about? The **stuff** that doctor in

Jacksonville gave you? Have you been putting that on?"

"Yes, sir," said Rob.

"Well," said Mr. Phelmer, "let me tell you what I think. Let me be **up-front** and honest with you. I think it might be a good idea if we had you stay home for a few days. What we'll do is just give that old medicine more of a chance to **kick in,** let it start working its magic on you, and then we'll have you come back to school when your legs have cleared up. What do you think about that plan?"

Rob stared down at his legs. He felt the picture of the tiger burning in his pocket. He **concentrate**d on keeping his heart from singing out loud with joy.

"Yes, sir," he said slowly, "that would be all right."

"That's right," said Mr. Phelmer. "I thought you would think it's a good plan. I'll tell you what I'll do. I'll just write your parents—I mean your father—a note, and tell him what's what; he can give me a call if he wants. We can talk about it."

"Yes, sir," said Rob again. He kept his head down. He was afraid to look up.

Mr. Phelmer cleared his throat and **scratch**ed his head and **adjust**ed his piece of hair, and then he started to write.

When he was done, he handed the note to Rob; Rob took it, and when he was outside the principal's office, he folded the piece of paper up carefully and put it in his back pocket with the drawing of the tiger.

And then, finally, he smiled. He smiled because he knew something Mr. Phelmer did not know. He knew that his legs would never clear up.

He was free.

Rob **float**ed through the rest of the morning. He went to maths class and civics★ and science, his heart light, **buoy**ed by the knowledge that he would never have to come back.

At lunch, he sat out on the benches in the breezeway.✳ He did not go into the lunchroom; Norton and Billy Threemonger were there. And nothing had tasted good to him since his mother died, especially not the food at the school. It was worse than the food his father tried to cook.

He sat on the bench and **unfold**ed his drawing of the tiger, and his fingers **itch**ed to start making it in wood. He was sitting like that, **swing**ing his legs, studying the drawing, when he heard shouting and the **high-pitched buzz** of excitement, like **crickets**, that the kids made when

---

★ civics 정치학.
✳ breezeway 떨어진 건물 사이를 잇는 지붕과 기둥만 있는 복도.

something was happening.

He stayed where he was. In a minute, the **fade**d red double doors of the lunchroom swung open and Sistine Bailey came **march**ing through them, her head held high. Behind her was a whole group of kids, and just when Sistine noticed Rob sitting there on the bench, one of the kids threw something at her; Rob couldn't tell what. But it hit her, whatever it was.

"Run!" he wanted to **yell** at her. "Hurry up and run!"

But he didn't say anything. He knew better than to say anything. He just sat and stared at Sistine with his mouth open, and she stared back at him. Then she turned and walked back into the group of kids, like somebody walking into deep water.

And suddenly, she began swinging with her **fist**s. She was kicking. She was **twirl**ing. Then the group of kids closed in around her and she seemed to disappear. Rob stood up so that he could see her better. He caught sight of her pink dress; it looked all **crumple**d, like a **wad**ded-up tissue.

He saw her arms still going like mad.

"Hey!" he shouted, not meaning to.

"Hey!" he shouted again, louder. He moved closer, the drawing of the tiger still in his hand.

"Leave her alone!" he shouted, not believing that the

words were coming from him.

They heard him then and turned to him. It was quiet for a minute.

"Who you talking to?" a big girl with black hair asked.

"Yeah," another girl said. "Who do you think you're talking to?"

"Go away," Sistine **mutter**ed in her **gravelly** voice. But she didn't look at him. Her yellow hair was **stuck** to her **forehead** with **sweat**.

The girl with the black hair pushed up close to him. She **shove**d him.

"Leave her alone," Rob said again.

"You going to make me?" the black-haired girl said.

They were all looking at him. Waiting. Sistine was waiting, too; waiting for him to do something. He looked down at the ground and saw what they had thrown at her. It was an apple. He stared at it for what seemed like a long time, and when he looked back up, they were all still waiting to see what he would do.

And so he ran. And after a minute, he could tell that they were running after him; he didn't need to look back to see if they were there. He knew it. He knew the feeling of being **chased**. He dropped the picture of the tiger and ran full out, **pump**ing his legs and arms hard. They were still behind him. A sudden **thrill** went through him when he realized that what he was doing was saving Sistine Bailey.

Why he would try to save Sistine Bailey, why he would want to save somebody who hated him, he couldn't say. He just ran, and the bell rang before they caught him. He was late for his English class because he had to walk from the **gym** all the way to the front of the school. And he did not know where his drawing of the tiger was, but he still had Mr. Phelmer's note in his back pocket and that was all that truly **matter**ed to him, the note that proved that he would never have to come back.

chapter

7

It **turned out** to be an **extraordinary** day in almost every possible way. It started with finding the tiger, and it ended with Sistine Bailey sitting down next to him on the bus on the way home from school. Her dress was **torn** and **muddied**. There was a **scrape** down her right arm, and her hair stuck out in a hundred different directions. She sat down in the empty seat beside him and **stared** at him with her black eyes.

"There isn't any place else to sit," she said to him. "This is the last empty seat."

Rob **shrugged**.

"It's not like I want to sit here," she said.

"Okay," said Rob. He shrugged his shoulders again. He hoped she wasn't going to thank him for saving her.

"What's your name?" she **demanded**.

"Rob Horton," he told her.

"Well, let me tell you something, Rob Horton. You shouldn't run. That's what they want you to do. Run."

Rob stared at her with his mouth open. She stared back.

"I hate it here," she said, looking away from him, her voice even deeper than before. "This is a stupid **hick** town with stupid hick teachers. Nobody in the whole school even knows what the Sistine Chapel is."

"I know," said Rob. "I know what the Sistine Chapel is." **Immediately**, he **regret**ted saying it. It was his **policy** not to say things, but it was a policy he was having a hard time **maintain**ing around Sistine.

"I **bet**," Sistine **sneer**ed at him. "I bet you know."

"It's a picture of God making the world," he said.

Sistine stared at him hard. She **narrow**ed her small eyes until they almost disappeared.

"It's in Italy," said Rob. "The pictures are painted on the **ceiling**. They're frescoes.*" It was as if a magician had cast a **spell** over him. He opened his mouth and the words fell out, once on top of the other, like gold coins. He couldn't stop talking. "I don't got to go to school **on account of** my legs. I got a note that says so. Mr. Phelmer—he's the

---

★ fresco [미술] 프레스코화. 석회를 바른 벽에 그것이 마르기 전에 그림을 그리는 화법.

principal—he says the parents are worried that what I got is **contagious**. That means that the other kids could catch it."

"I know what *contagious* means," Sistine said. She looked at his legs. And then she did something truly **astound**ing: she closed her eyes and reached out her left hand and placed it on top of Rob's right leg.

"Please let me catch it," she **whisper**ed.

"You won't," said Rob, surprised at her hand, how small it was and how warm. It made him think, for a minute, of his mother's hand, tiny and soft. He stopped that thought. "It ain't contagious," he told her.

"Please let me catch it," Sistine whispered again, **ignoring** him, keeping her hand on his leg. "Please let me catch it so I won't have to go to school."

"It ain't a **disease**," said Rob. "It's just me."

"Shut up," Sistine said. She sat up very straight. Her lips moved. The other kids shouted and screamed and laughed and called to each other, but the two of them sat **apart** from it all, as if their seat was an island in the sea of **sweat** and **exhaust**.

Sistine opened her eyes. She took her hand away and **rub**bed it up and down both of her own legs.

"You're crazy," Rob told her.

"Where do you live?" Sistine asked, still rubbing her

hand over her legs.

"In the motel. In the Kentucky Star."

"You live in a motel?" she said, looking up at him.

"It ain't **permanent**," he told her. "It's just until we get back **on our feet**."

Sistine stared at him. "I'll bring you your homework," she said. "I'll bring it to you at the motel."

"I don't want my homework," he told her.

"So?" said Sistine.

By then, Norton and Billy Threemonger had **spot**ted them sitting together and they were moving in. Rob was **relieve**d when the first **thump** came to the back of his head, because it meant that he wouldn't have to talk to Sistine any more. It meant that he wouldn't **end up** saying too much, telling her about important things, like his mother or the tiger. He was glad, almost, that Norton and Billy were there to **beat** him into silence.

His father read the note from the principal slowly, putting his big finger under the words as if they were bugs he was trying to keep **still**. When he was finally done, he laid the letter on the table and **rub**bed his eyes with his fingers and **sigh**ed. The rain beat a sad **rhythm** on the roof of the motel.

"That **stuff** ain't nothing anybody else can catch," his father said.

"I know it," Rob told him.

"I already told that to that **principal** once before. I called up there and told him that."

"Yes, sir," said Rob.

His father sighed. He stopped rubbing his eyes and looked up at Rob. "You want to stay home?" he asked.

Rob **nod**ded.

His father sighed again. "Maybe I'll make an **appointment**, get one of them doctors to write down that what you got ain't catching. All right?"

"Yes, sir," said Rob.

"But I won't do it for a few days. I'll give you some time off."

"That would be all right," said Rob.

"You got to fight them, you know. Them boys. I know you don't want to. But you got to fight them, else they won't ever leave you alone."

Rob nodded. He saw Sistine **twirl**ing and **punch**ing and kicking, and the **vision** made him smile.

"**In the meantime**, you can help me out around here," his father said. "Do some of the **maintenance**-man work at the motel, do some **sweep**ing and cleaning for me. Beauchamp's running me **ragged**. There ain't enough hours in the day to do everything that man wants done. Now go on and hand me that medicine."

His father **slather**ed and **slap**ped the **fishy**-smelling **ointment** on Rob's legs, and Rob concentrated on holding still.

"Do you think Beauchamp is the richest man in the world?" he asked his father.

"Naw," his father said. "He don't own but this one itty-bitty* motel now. And the woods. He just likes to **pretend** he's rich is all. Why?"

"I was just wondering," said Rob. He was thinking about the tiger **pacing** back and forth in the cage. He was certain that the tiger belonged to Beauchamp, and wouldn't you have to be the richest man in the world to own a tiger? Rob wanted, **desperate**ly, to go see the tiger again. But he was afraid that he had imagined the whole thing; he was afraid that the tiger might have disappeared with the morning **mist**.

"Can I go outside?" Rob asked when his father was done.

"Naw," his father said. "I don't want that medicine **rain**ed off you. It cost too much."

Rob was **relieve**d, almost, that he had to stay inside. What if he went looking for the tiger and he was not there?

Rob's father cooked them macaroni and cheese* for **supper** on the two-burner hot plate* they kept on the table next to the TV. He boiled the macaroni too long and a lot of it **stuck** to the pan, so there weren't many noodles to go with the **powdery** cheese.

"Someday," he told Rob, "you and me will have a house

★ itty-bitty (= itsy-bitsy) 작은, 조그마한.
✳ macaroni and cheese 치즈 소스에 마카로니를 넣고 구운 요리.
✺ hot plate 요리용 철판.

with a real **stove**, and I'll do some good cooking then."

"This is good," Rob lied.

"You eat all you want. I ain't that hungry," his father told him.

After supper, his father fell asleep in the **recliner**, with his head thrown back and his mouth open. He **snored**, and his feet—big, with **crooked** toes—**jerk**ed and **trembled**. In between the snores, his stomach **growl**ed long and loud, as if he was the hungriest man in the world.

Rob sat on his bed and started to work on **carving** the tiger. He had a good piece of maple* and his knife was sharp, and in his mind he could see the tiger clearly. But something different came out of the wood. It wasn't a tiger at all. It was a person, with a sharp nose and small eyes and **skinny** legs. It wasn't until he started working on the dress that Rob realized he was carving Sistine.

He stopped for a minute and held the wood out in front of him and shook his head in wonder. It was just like his mother had always said: you could never tell what would come out of the wood. It did what it wanted and you just followed.

He **stay**ed **up** late working on the carving, and when he finally fell asleep he dreamed about the tiger, only it

---

★ maple 단풍나무.

wasn't in a cage. It was free and running through the woods, and there was something on its back, but Rob couldn't tell what it was. As the tiger got closer and closer, Rob saw that the thing was Sistine in her pink party dress. She was riding the tiger. In his dream, Rob **wave**d to her and she waved back at him. But she didn't stop. She and the tiger kept going, past Rob, deeper and deeper into the woods.

chapter

9

His father woke him up at five-thirty the next morning.

"Come on, son," he said, shaking Rob's shoulder. "Come on; you're a working man now. You got to get up." He took his hand away and stood over Rob for a minute more, and then he left.

Rob heard the door to the motel room **squeak** open. He opened his eyes. The world was dark. The only light came from the falling Kentucky Star. Rob turned over in bed and pulled back the curtain and looked out the window at the sign. It was like having his own **personal shooting star**, but he didn't ever make a wish on it. He was afraid that if he started wishing, he might not be able to stop. In his **suitcase** of not-thoughts, there were also not-wishes. He kept the **lid** closed on them, too.

Rob **lean**ed on his **elbow** and stared at the star and

listened to the rain gently **drum**ming its fingers on the roof. There was a warm **glow**ing kind of feeling in his stomach, a feeling that he wasn't used to. It took him a minute to name it. The tiger. The tiger was out there. He got out of bed and put on shorts and a T-shirt.

"Still hot," his father said, when Rob stepped out the door. "And still raining."

"Uh-huh," said Rob, **rub**bing his eyes, "yes, sir."

"If it don't stop soon, the whole state ain't going to be nothing but one big **swamp**."

"The rain don't **bother** me," Rob **mutter**ed.

On the day of his mother's **funeral**, it had been so sunshiny that it hurt his eyes. And after the funeral, he and his father had to stand outside in the hot, bright light and shake everybody's hand. Some of the ladies hugged Rob, pulling him to them in **jerky**, **desperate** movements, **smash**ing his head into their **pillow**y chests.

"If you don't look just like her," they told him, **rock**ing him back and forth and holding on to him tight.

Or they said, "You got your mama's hair—that **cobweb**by blond," and they ran their fingers through his hair and **pat**ted his head like he was a dog.

And every time Rob's father **extend**ed his hand to somebody else, Rob saw the **rip**ped place in his suit, where it had **split** open when he **slap**ped Rob to make him stop

36

crying. And it **remind**ed Rob again: *Do not cry. Do not cry.*

That was what the sun made him think of. The funeral. And so he didn't care if he ever saw the sun again. He didn't care if the whole state *did* turn into a swamp.

His father stood up and went back into the motel room and got himself a cup of coffee and brought it back outside. The **steam** rose off it and **curl**ed into the air.

"Now that I'm a working man," Rob said shyly, "could I drink some coffee?"

His father smiled at him. "Well," he said, "I guess that'd be all right."

Rob went inside and poured himself a mug of coffee and brought it back outside and sat down next to his father and **sip**ped it slowly. It tasted hot and dark and **bitter**. He liked it.

"All right," his father said after about ten minutes, "it's time to get to work." He stood up. It wasn't even six o'clock.

As they walked together alongside the back of the motel to the **maintenance shed**, his father started to **whistle** "**Mining** for Gold." It was a sad song he used to sing with Rob's mother. Her high sweet voice had gone **swoop**ing over his father's deep one, like a small bird flying over the **solid** world.

His father must have remembered, too, because he stopped halfway through the song and shook his head and cursed softly under his breath.

Rob let his father walk ahead of him. He slowed down and stared into the woods, wanting to see some small part of the tiger, a **flick** of his tail or the glow from his eyes. But there was nothing to see except for rain and darkness.

"Come on, son," his father said, his voice hard. And Rob hurried to **catch up**.

chapter

10

Rob was **sweep**ing the **laundry** room when Willie May, the Kentucky Star's **housekeeper**, came in and threw herself down in one of the metal chairs that were lined up against the cement-block wall.

"You know what?" she said to Rob.

"No, ma'am," said Rob.

"I tell you what," said Willie May. She reached up and **adjust**ed the butterfly clip in her thick black hair. "I'd rather be sweeping up after some pigs in a **barn** than cleaning up after the people in this place. Pigs at least give you some **respect**."

Rob leaned on his **broom** and stared at Willie May. He liked looking at her. Her face was **smooth** and dark, like a beautiful piece of wood. And Rob liked to think that if he had been the one who **carved** Willie May, he would have made her just the way she was, with her long nose and high **cheekbone**s and **slant**ed eyes.

"What you staring at?" Willie May asked. Her eyes **narrow**ed. "What you doing out of school?"

Rob **shrug**ged. "I don't know," he said.

"What you mean, you don't know?"

Rob shrugged again.

"Don't be moving your shoulders up and down in front of me, acting like some **skinny** old bird trying to fly away. You want to **end up** cleaning motel rooms for a living?"

Rob shook his head.

"That's right. Ain't nobody wants this job. I'm the only fool Beauchamp can pay to do it. You got to stay in school," she said, "else you'll end up like me." She shook her head and reached into the pocket of her dress and pulled out a single **cigarette** and two sticks of Eight Ball licorice★ gum. She put one piece of gum in her mouth, handed the other one to Rob, **lit** her cigarette, leaned back in the chair and closed her eyes. "Now," she said. The **scent** of smoke and licorice slowly filled the laundry room. "Go on and tell me why you ain't in school."

"**On account of** my legs being all broke out," said Rob.

Willie May opened her eyes and looked over the top of

★ licorice 감초. 약이나 과자의 원료로 사용한다.

her glasses at Rob's legs.

"Mmmm," she said after a minute. "How long you had that?"

"About six months," said Rob.

"I can tell you how to **cure** that," said Willie May, pointing with her cigarette at his legs. "I can tell you right now. Don't need to go to no doctor."

"Huh?" said Rob. He stopped **chew**ing his gum and held his breath. What if Willie May **heal**ed him and then he had to go back to school?

"Sadness," said Willie May, closing her eyes and nodding her head. "You keeping all that sadness down low, in your legs. You not letting it get up to your heart, where it belongs. You got to let that sadness rise on up."

"Oh," said Rob. He let his breath out. He was **relieve**d. Willie May was wrong. She couldn't cure him.

"The **principal** thinks it's **contagious**," he said.

"Man ain't got no sense," Willie May said.

"He's got lots of **certificates**," Rob **offer**ed. "They're all **frame**d and hung up on his wall."

"I **bet** he ain't got no certificate for sense though," said Willie May darkly. She rose up out of her chair and **stretch**ed. "I got to clean some rooms," she said. "You ain't going to forget what I told you 'bout them legs, are you?"

"No, ma'am," said Rob.

"What'd I tell you then?" she said, **tower**ing over him. Willie May was tall, the tallest person Rob had ever seen.

"To let the sadness rise," Rob said. He repeated the words as if they were part of a **poem**. He gave them a certain **rhythm**, the same way Willie May had when she said them.

"That's right," said Willie May. "You got to let the sadness rise on up."

She left the room in a **swirl** of licorice and smoke; after she was gone, Rob wished that he had told her about the tiger. He felt a sudden desperate need to tell somebody—somebody who wouldn't **doubt** him. Somebody who was **capable** of believing in tigers.

chapter

11

That afternoon, Rob was out in front of the Kentucky Star, **weed**ing between the **cracks** in the **sidewalk**, when the school bus **rumble**d up.

"Hey!" he heard Norton Threemonger **yell**. Rob didn't look up. He **concentrate**d on the weeds.

"Hey, **disease** boy!" Norton shouted. "We know what you got. It's called leprosy.★"

"Yeah!" Billy shouted. "Leprosy. All of your body parts are going to fall off."

"They're going to *rot* off!" Norton yelled.

"Yeah!" Billy screamed. "That's what I meant. Rot. They're going to rot off."

Rob **stare**d at the sidewalk and imagined the tiger eating

★leprosy 나병. 나균에 의해 감염되는 만성 전염성 질환.

Norton and Billy Threemonger and then **spit**ting out their bones.

"Hey!" Norton shouted. "Here comes your girlfriend, disease boy."

The bus **cough**ed and **sputter**ed and finally **roar**ed away. Rob looked up. Sistine was walking toward him. She was wearing a lime green dress. As she got closer, he could see that it was **torn** and dirty.

"I brought your homework," she said. She held out a red notebook **stuff**ed full of papers. The **knuckle**s on her hand were **bleed**ing.

"Thank you," said Rob. He took the notebook. He was **determined** to say nothing else to her. He was determined to keep his words inside himself, where they belonged.

Sistine stared past him at the motel. It was an ugly two-**story** building, **squat** and small, **composed entirely** of cement block. The doors of each room were painted a different color, pink or blue or green, and there was a chair, painted in a matching color, sitting in front of each door.

"Why is this place called the Kentucky Star?" Sistine asked.

"Because," said Rob. It was the shortest answer he could think of.

"Because why?" she asked.

Rob **sigh**ed. "Because Beauchamp, the man who owns it, he had a horse once, called Kentucky Star."

44

"Well," said Sistine, "it's a stupid name for a hotel in Florida."

Rob shrugged.

It started to rain; Sistine stood in front of him and continued to stare. She looked at the motel and then over at the **blink**ing Kentucky Star sign, and then she looked back at him, as if it was all a maths **equation** she was trying to make come out right in her head.

The rain made her hair **stick** to her **scalp**. It made her dress **droopy**. Rob looked at her small **pinched** face and her bleeding knuckles and dark eyes, and he felt something inside of him open up. It was the same way he felt when he picked up a piece of wood and started working on it, not knowing what it would be and then watching it turn into something he **recognize**d.

He took a breath. He opened his mouth and let the words fall out. "I know where there's a tiger."

Sistine stood in the **drizzly** rain and stared at him, her eyes black and **fierce**.

She didn't say "A real one?"

She didn't say "Are you crazy?"

She didn't say "You're a big old liar."

She said one word: "*Where?*"

And Rob knew then that he had picked the right person to tell.

chapter

12

"We got to walk through the woods," Rob said. He looked
doubtfully at Sistine's bright dress and shiny black shoes.

"You can give me some of your clothes to wear," she
told him. "I hate this dress, anyway."

And so he took her to the motel room, and there Sistine
stood and stared at the **unmade** beds and the **tattered**
recliner. Her eyes moved over his father's gun case and
then went to the macaroni pan from the night before, still
sitting on the hot plate. She looked at it all the same way
she had looked at the Kentucky Star sign and the motel and
him, like she was trying to add it up in her head.

Then she saw his carvings, the little wooden village of
odd things that he had made. He had them all on a TV
dinner* tray beside his bed.

"Oh," she said—her voice sounded different, lighter—

"where did you get those?"

She went and **bent** over the tray and studied the carvings, the blue jay* and the pine tree* and the Kentucky Star sign and the one that he was **particularly** proud of, his father's right foot, **life-size** and **accurate** right down to the little toe. She picked them up one by one and then placed them back down carefully.

"Where did you get them?" she asked again.

"I made 'em," said Rob.

She did not doubt him, as some people would. Instead, she said, "Michelangelo*—the man who painted the Sistine ceiling—he **sculpt**ed, too. You're a **sculptor**," she said. "You're an artist."

"Naw," said Rob. He shook his head. He felt a hot **wave** of **embarrass**ment and joy roll over him. It **lit** his **rash** on fire. He bent and **rub**bed his hands down his legs, trying to calm them. When he **straighten**ed back up, he saw that Sistine had picked up the carving of her. He had left it **lying** on his bed, **intend**ing to work on it again in the evening.

He held his breath as she stared at the piece of wood. It

★ TV dinner 전자레인지에 데우기만 하면 한 끼 식사로 먹을 수 있게 포장해서 파는 냉동 식품. TV를 보면서 간단히 먹을 수 있다고 해서 이런 이름을 붙였다.
✻ jay 어치. 까마귓과의 새.
✻ pine tree 소나무.
✻Michelangelo 미켈란젤로. 이탈리아의 조각가·화가·건축가·시인.

looked so much like her, with her skinny legs and small eyes and **defiant stance**, that he was certain she would be angry. But once again she surprised him.

"Oh," she said, her voice full of wonder, "it's perfect. It's like looking in a little wooden mirror." She stared at it a minute more and then carefully laid it back on his bed.

"Give me some clothes," she said, "and we'll go see the tiger."

He gave her a pair of pants and a T-shirt, and left the room and went outside to wait for her.

It was still raining, but not hard. He looked at the falling Kentucky Star. He thought for a minute about one of the not-wishes he had **buried** deepest: a friend. He stared at the star and felt the hope and need and fear **course** through him in a hot neon **arc**. He shook his head.

"Naw," he said to the Kentucky Star. "Naw."

And then he **sigh**ed and **stuck** his legs out into the rain, hoping to cool them off, hoping to get some small amount of **relief.**

chapter

13

They walked together through the **scrub**. The rain had stopped, but the whole world was wet. The pines and the palmettos★ and the sad **cluster**s of dead orange trees all **drip**ped water.

"This is where my mother grew up," Sistine said, **swing**ing her arms wide as she walked. "Right here in Lister. And she said that she always told herself that if she ever **made it** out of here, she wasn't going to come back. But now she's back because my father had an **affair** with his **secretary**, whose name is Bridgette and who can't **type**, which is a really bad thing for a secretary not to be able to do. And my mother left him when she found out. He's coming down here to get me. Soon. Next week, probably.

★ **palmetto** 팔메토. 미국 동남부산 작은 야자나무.

I'm going to live with him. I'm not staying here, that's for sure."

Rob felt a familiar loneliness rise up and **drape** its arm over his shoulder. She wasn't staying. There was no point in wishing; the **suitcase** needed to stay closed. He stared at Sistine's shiny shoes and **will**ed his sadness to go away.

"Ain't you worried about **mess**ing **up** your shoes?" he asked her.

"No," she said, "I hate these shoes. I hate every piece of clothing that my mother makes me wear. Does your mother live with you?"

Rob shook his head. "Naw," he said.

"Where is she?"

Rob **shrugg**ed his shoulders.

"My mother's going to open up a store downtown. It's going to be an art store. She's going to bring some culture to the area. She could sell some of your wood **sculpture**s."

"They ain't sculptures," Rob **protest**ed. "They're just **whittling**. That's all. And we got to be quiet because Beauchamp don't want people walking around on his land."

"Is this his land?" Sistine asked.

"Everything's his," said Rob. "The motel and these woods."

"He can't own everything," Sistine **argue**d. "Besides,"

she said, "I don't care. He can catch us. He can put us in **jail** for **trespass**ing. I don't care."

"If we're in jail, we won't get to see the tiger," said Rob.

"Where's your mother?" Sistine **demand**ed suddenly. She stopped walking and stared at him.

"Shhh," said Rob. "You got to be quiet." He kept walking.

"I do not have to be quiet," Sistine called after him. "I want to know where your mother is."

He turned around and looked at her. Her hands were on her hips. Her black eyes were **narrow**ed.

"I don't want to see your stupid tiger!" she shouted. "I don't care about it. You don't know how to talk to people. I told you about my father and my mother and Bridgette, and you didn't say anything. You won't even tell me about your mother." Keeping her hands on her hips, she turned around and started **march**ing back in the direction of the Kentucky Star. "Keep your stupid secrets!" she shouted. "Keep your stupid tiger, too. I don't care."

Rob watched her. Because she was wearing his jeans and his shirt, it was like looking into a fun-house★ mirror. It was like watching himself walk away. He shrugged and **bent** to **scratch** his legs. He told himself that he didn't care.

★ fun-house 놀이공원의 유령의 집.

He told himself that she was leaving soon, anyway.

But when he looked up and saw her getting smaller and smaller, it **remind**ed him of his dream. He remembered Sistine riding into the woods on the back of the tiger. And suddenly, he couldn't **bear** the thought of watching her disappear again.

"Wait up!" he shouted. "Wait up!" And he started to run toward her.

Sistine turned and stopped. She waited for him with her hands on her hips.

"Well?" she said when he got close to her.

"She's dead," he told her. The words came out in short, **ragged gasp**s. "My mama's dead."

"Okay," said Sistine. She gave a quick, **professional nod** of her head. She stepped toward him. And Rob turned. And together they walked back in the other direction, toward the tiger.

chapter

14

The cage was made out of **rust**ed chainlink fence;★ there was a wooden **board** that **serv**ed as a roof and there was a chainlink door that was locked tight with three **padlock**s. Inside the cage, the tiger was still **pacing** back and forth, just as he had been the last time Rob saw him, as if he had never stopped pacing, or as if Rob had never gone away.

"Oh," said Sistine in the same voice that she had used when she saw Rob's **carving**s. "He's beautiful."

"Don't get too close," Rob **order**ed. "He might not like it if you stand too close."

But the tiger **ignore**d them. He **concentrate**d on pacing. He was so **enormous** and bright that it was hard to look directly at him.

★ chainlink fence 굵은 철사를 다이아몬드 모양으로 엮은 울타리.

"It's just like the **poem** says," Sistine breathed.

"What?" said Rob.

"That poem. The one that goes, 'Tiger, tiger, burning bright, in the forests of the night.' That poem. It's just like that. He burns bright."

"Oh," said Rob. He nodded. He liked the **fierce** and beautiful way the words sounded. Just as he was getting ready to ask Sistine to say them again, she **whirl**ed around and **face**d him.

"What's he doing way out here?" she demanded.

Rob shrugged. "I don't know," he said. "He's Beauchamp's, I guess."

"Beauchamp's what?" said Sistine. "His pet?"

"I don't know," said Rob. "I just like looking at him. Maybe Beauchamp does, too. Maybe he just likes to come out here and look at him."

"That's **selfish**," said Sistine.

Rob shrugged.

"This isn't right, for this tiger to be in a cage. It's not right."

"We can't do nothing about it," Rob said.

"We could let him go," said Sistine. "We could **set** him **free**." She put her hands on her hips. It was a **gesture** that Rob had already come to **recognize** and be **wary** of.

"We can't," he said. "There's all them locks."

"We can **saw** through them."

"Naw," said Rob. The **mere** thought of letting the tiger go made his legs **itch** like crazy.

"We have to set him free," Sistine said, her voice loud and certain.

"Nuh-uh," said Rob. "It ain't our tiger to let go."

"It's our tiger to save," Sistine said fiercely.

The tiger stopped pacing. He **prick**ed **his ears** back and forth, looking somewhere past Sistine and Rob.

"Shhh," said Rob.

The tiger **cock**ed his head. All three of them listened.

"It's a car," said Rob. "A car's coming. It's Beauchamp. We got to go. Come on."

He **grab**bed her hand and pulled her into the woods. She ran with him. She let him hold on to her hand. It was an impossibly small and **bony** hand, as **delicate** as the **skeleton** of a baby bird.

They ran together, and Rob felt his heart move inside him—not from fear or **exertion** but from something else. It was as if his soul had grown and was pushing everything up higher in his body. It was an **odd**ly familiar feeling, but he couldn't remember what it was called.

"Is he behind us?" Sistine asked **breathless**ly.

Rob shrugged; it was hard to move his shoulders up and down and keep hold of Sistine's hand at the same time.

Sistine said, "Stop shrugging your shoulders at me. I hate it. I hate the way you shrug all the time."

And that made Rob remember Willie May saying that when he shrugged he looked like a **skinny** bird trying to fly. It **struck** him as funny now. He laughed out loud at the thought of it. And without asking him what he was laughing about, without dropping his hand, without stopping, Sistine laughed, too.

Then Rob remembered the name of the feeling that was pushing up inside him, filling him full to **overflow**ing. It was happiness. That was what it was called.

chapter

15

By the time they **made it** back to the motel **parking lot**, it was dark outside, and they were both laughing so hard that they could **barely** walk.

"Rob?" said his father. He was standing at the door to their room. The blue-gray light from inside **seep**ed out around him.

"Yes, sir," said Rob. He dropped Sistine's hand. He stood up straight.

"Where you been?"

"Out in the woods."

"Did you finish up all them jobs I told you to do?"

"Yes, sir," said Rob.

"Who you got with you?" his father said, **squint**ing into the darkness.

Sistine drew herself up tall.

Chapter Fifteen

57

"This is Sistine," said Rob.

"Uh-huh," said his father, still squinting. "You live around here?" he asked.

"For now," said Sistine.

"Your parents know you're out here?"

"I was going to call my mother," said Sistine.

"There's a pay phone★ down in the **laundry** room," said Rob's father.

"In the laundry room?" Sistine repeated, her voice full of **disbelief**. She put her hands on her hips.

"We don't got a phone in the room," Rob said to her softly.

"Good grief,✷" said Sistine. "Well, can I have some **change** at least?"

Rob's father reached into his pants pocket and pulled out a **handful** of coins. He balanced the money in the **palm** of his hand, as if he was preparing to do a magic **trick**, and Rob stepped forward and took the coins from him and handed them to Sistine.

"You want me to go with you?" he asked her.

"No," she said. "I'll find it. Thank you very much."

"Rob," his father said as Sistine **march**ed away swinging her arms, "what's that girl doing in your clothes?"

★ pay phone 주화를 넣는 공중 전화.
✷ good grief [감탄사] 어머나! 맙소사!

"She had on a dress," Rob said. "It was too pretty to wear out in the woods."

"Come on in here," his father **command**ed. "Let's get that medicine on your legs."

"Yes, sir," said Rob. He walked toward the room slowly. His happiness had **evaporate**d. His legs itched. And the motel room, he knew, would be as dark as a **cave**, **lit** only by the gray light of the TV.

When his mother was alive, the world had seemed full of light. The Christmas before she died, she had **strung** the outside of their house, in Jacksonville, with hundreds of white lights. Every night, the house lit up like a **constellation**, and they were all inside it together, the three of them. And they were happy.

Rob remembered and, as he remembered, he stepped into the motel room. He shook his head and **scold**ed himself for opening his suitcase. Just thinking about all the things that were gone now seemed to make the darkness darker.

chapter

16

Rob sat out on the **curb** in front of the motel room and waited for Sistine to come back from using the phone. He had her green dress **wrap**ped up in a **grocery** bag. He had tried to fold the dress up **neat**ly, but folding a dress **turn**ed **out** to be an impossible **task** and he finally **gave up**. Now he held the bag out and away from him, so that the **grease** from the medicine on his legs would not **stain** it.

He was **relieve**d when Sistine finally walked toward him out of the darkness. "Hey," he said.

"Hi." She sat down on the steps next to him. "How come you don't have a phone?"

Rob **shrug**ged. "Ain't got nobody to call, I guess."

"My mother's coming to get me," Sistine said.

Rob **nod**ded. "Here's your dress." He handed her the bag.

Sistine took it and then **tilt**ed her head to look up at the sky. Rob looked up, too. The clouds had **shift**ed, and there were clear **patch**es where the stars **shone** through.

"I can see the Big Dipper,*" Sistine said. "I like looking up at things. So do my mom and dad. That's how they met. They were both looking up at the **ceiling** in the Sistine Chapel and they weren't watching where they were going and they **bump**ed into each other. That's why I'm named Sistine."

"I like your name," said Rob shyly.

"I've seen the Sistine ceiling, too," she said. "They took me last year. Before Bridgette. When they were still in love."

"Does it look like the pictures?" Rob asked.

"Better," said Sistine. "It's like—I don't know—it's like looking at **firework**s, kind of."

"Oh," said Rob.

"Maybe we could go to Italy some time. And I could show you."

"That would be all right," said Rob. He smiled into the darkness.

"That tiger can't look up at the stars," said Sistine, her voice getting hard. "He's got that piece of wood over his

---

★ Big Dipper 북두칠성.

head. He can't look up at all. We've got to let him go."

Rob was silent. He was hoping that if he didn't answer her, she might go back to talking about the Sistine ceiling.

"How did your mother die?" she asked suddenly.

Rob **sigh**ed. He knew there was no point in trying not to answer. "**Cancer**," he said.

"What was her name?"

"I ain't supposed to talk about her," said Rob, closing his eyes to the stars and **concentrating** instead on his **suitcase**, working to keep it closed.

"Why not?" asked Sistine.

"Because. My dad says it don't do no good to talk about it. He says she's gone and she ain't coming back. That's why we moved here from Jacksonville. Because everybody always wanted to talk about her. We moved down here to get on with things."

There was the **crunch** of **gravel**. Rob opened his eyes **in time** to see the headlights of a car **sweep** over them.

"That's my mother," said Sistine. She stood up. "Quick," she said. "Tell me your mother's name."

Rob shook his head.

"Say it," she demanded.

"Caroline," Rob said softly, **crack**ing his suitcase open and letting the word **slip** out.

Sistine gave him another **businesslike** nod of her head.

"Okay," she said. "I'll come back tomorrow. And we'll make our plans for letting the tiger go."

"Sissy?" called a voice. "Baby, what in the world? What in the world are you doing out here?"

Sistine's mother got out of the car and came walking toward them. She had on high heels, and she **wobble**d as she walked in the gravel **parking lot** of the Kentucky Star. Her hair was a lighter **shade** of yellow than Sistine's and **pile**d up high. When she turned her head, Rob recognized Sistine's **profile**, her sharp **chin** and **pointed** nose, but the mouth was different, tighter.

"Good Lord,★" said Mrs. Bailey to Sistine. "What have you got on?"

"Clothes," said Sistine.

"Sissy, you look like a **hobo**. Get in the car." She **tap**ped her high-heeled foot on the gravel.

Sistine didn't move. She stood beside Rob.

"Well," said her mother when Sistine didn't move, "you must be Rob. What's your last name, Rob?"

"Horton," said Rob.

"Horton," said Mrs. Bailey. "Horton. Are you related to Seldon Horton, the **congressman**?"

"No, ma'am," said Rob. "I don't think so."

★ good Lord [감탄사] 하느님 맙소사!

Mrs. Bailey's eyes **flick**ed away from him and back to Sistine. "Baby," said Mrs. Bailey, "please get in the car."

When Sistine still didn't move, Mrs. Bailey sighed and looked back at Rob again. "She won't listen to a word I say," Mrs. Bailey told him. "Her father is the only one she'll listen to." And then under her breath she **mutter**ed, "Her father, the liar."

Sistine **growl**ed somewhere deep in her **throat** and **stalk**ed to the car and got in and **slam**med the door. "You're the liar!" she shouted from the back seat of the car. "You're the one who lies!"

"Jesus,★" said Mrs. Bailey. She shook her head and turned and walked back to the car without saying anything else to Rob.

Rob watched them **pull away**. He could see Sistine sitting in the back seat. Her shoulders were **slump**ed.

A motel room door slammed. Somebody laughed. A dog barked once, short and high, and then stopped. And then there was silence.

"Caroline," Rob **whisper**ed into the darkness. "Caroline. Caroline. Caroline." The word was as sweet as **forbid**den candy on his tongue.

★ Jesus [감탄사] 이크! 예수님을 뜻하지만 놀람을 나타내는 감탄사로 사용된다.

chapter

17

The next morning, Rob was helping Willie May in the laundry room. They were folding sheets and chewing Eight Ball gum.

All night, he had tossed and turned, scratching his legs and thinking about the tiger and what Sistine said, that he had to be set free. He had finally decided to get Willie May's opinion.

"You ever been to a zoo?" Rob asked her.

"One time," said Willie May. She cracked her gum. "Went to that zoo over in Sorley. Place stunk."

"Do you think them animals minded it? Being locked up?"

"Wasn't nobody asking them did they mind." Willie May pulled another sheet out of the dryer and snapped it open.

Rob tried again. "Do you think it's bad to keep animals locked up?"

Willie May looked at him over the top of her glasses. She **stare**d at him hard.

Rob looked down at his feet.

"When I wasn't but little," said Willie May, "my daddy brought me a bird in a cage. It was a green parakeet bird.★ That bird was so small, I could hold it right in the **palm** of my hand." She **drape**d the sheet over one shoulder and held out a **cup**ped hand to show Rob. It looked to him like a hand big enough to hold the **entire** world.

"Held him in my hand. Could feel his little heart **beat**ing. He would look at me, **cock** his head this way and that. Called him Cricket, **on account of** him all the time singing."

"What happened to him?" Rob asked. Willie May **bent** and took a **pillow**case out of the dryer.

"Let him go," she said.

"You let him go?" Rob repeated, his heart **sink**ing inside him like a stone.

"Couldn't **stand** seeing him locked up, so I let him go." She folded the pillowcase carefully.

"And then what happened?"

★ parakeet bird 작은 잉꼬, 앵무새.

"I got beat by my daddy. He said I didn't do that bird no **favor**. Said all I did was give some snake its **supper**."

"So you never saw him again?" Rob asked.

"Nuh-uh," said Willie May. "But sometimes he comes flying through my dreams, **flit**ting about and singing." She shook her head and reached for the sheet on her shoulder. "Here," she said. "Go on and **grab** ahold of the other end. Help me fold this up."

Rob took hold of the sheet and, as it **billow**ed out between them, a memory rose up before him: his father standing out in the yard, holding his gun up to the sky, taking **aim** at a bird.

"You think I can hit it?" his father said. "You think I can hit that itty-bitty bird?"

"Robert," his mother said, "what do you want to shoot that bird for?"

"To prove I can," said his father.

There was a single crack and the bird was **suspend**ed in **midair**, **pin**ned for a moment to the sky with his father's **bullet**. Then it fell.

"Oh, Robert," his mother said.

It hurt the back of Rob's throat to think about that now, to think about the gun and his mother and the small *thud* the bird made when it hit the ground.

"I know something that's in a cage," said Rob, pushing

the words past the tightness in his throat.

Willie May nodded her head, but she wasn't listening. She was looking past Rob, past the white sheet, past the laundry room, past the Kentucky Star.

"Who don't?" she said finally. "Who don't know something in a cage?"

After that, they folded the sheets in silence. Rob thought about the bird and how when he had finally found its small still-warm body, he had started to cry.

His father told him not to.

"It ain't nothing to cry over," he'd said. "It's just a bird."

chapter

18

Rob was **sweep**ing the cement **walkway** in front of the Kentucky Star rooms when Beauchamp **pull**ed **up** in his red jeep and **honk**ed the **horn**.

"Hey there," he **holler**ed. Beauchamp was a large man with orange hair and an orange **beard** and a **permanent toothpick** in the side of his mouth. The toothpick **waggle**d as he talked, as if it was trying to make a point of its own. "We got you on the payroll★ now, too?" Beauchamp shouted.

"No, sir," said Rob.

"All right," **hoot**ed Beauchamp. He **hopp**ed out of the jeep. "Got you working for free. That's what I like to hear."

"Yes, sir," said Rob.

★ payroll 종업원 명부.

"Ain't you supposed to be in school? Or you done **graduate**d already?" The gold chains **buried** deep in Beauchamp's orange chest-hair **wink**ed at Rob.

"I'm sick," said Rob.

"Sick and tired of school, right?" He **slap**ped Rob on the back. "Don't got a mama putting down the rules for you, do you? Get to make your own rules. Not me," said Beauchamp. He **jerk**ed his head in the direction of the motel office, where his mother, Ida Belle, worked the front desk.

He winked at Rob and then looked to the left, then right. "Look here," he said in a quieter voice. "I've got me a number of deals going on right now, a few more than I can properly **handle**. I wonder if a smart boy like yourself wouldn't be looking for a way to pick up some extra **spending money**."

He didn't wait for Rob to answer.

"Let me tell you what I got cooking. You like animals?"

Rob nodded.

"Course you do," said Beauchamp, nodding with him. "What boy don't? You like wild animals?"

Rob's heart **skip**ped. He suddenly knew where Beauchamp was headed.

"I got me a wild animal," said Beauchamp. "I got me a wild animal like you would not believe. Right here on my own **property**. And I got some plans for him. Big plans. But **in the meantime**, he needs some taking care of, some daily **maintenance**. You following me, son?"

"Yes, sir," said Rob.

"All right," said Beauchamp. He slapped Rob on the shoulder again. "Why don't you climb on into this jeep and let me take you for a ride, show you what I'm talking about."

"I'm supposed to be sweeping," said Rob. He held up the **broom**.

"Says who?" said Beauchamp, suddenly angry. "Your daddy? He ain't the boss. *I'm* the boss. And if I say 'Let's go,' you say 'All right.'"

"All right," said Rob. He looked over his shoulder, wishing **fervent**ly that Willie May or his father would appear to save him from Beauchamp, knowing at the same time that he could not be saved, that he was on his own.

"Good," said Beauchamp. "Climb on up."

Rob climbed into the **passenger** seat. There was a big brown **grocery** bag at his feet.

"Go on and put that in the back," said Beauchamp as he **swung** into the driver's seat.

The bag was heavy and it **stunk**. Rob carefully put it on the floor in the back and then noticed his hands. There was blood on his fingers.

"That's just from the meat," said Beauchamp. "It won't hurt you none." He **crank**ed the engine. It **roar**ed to life, and they went **tear**ing around behind the Kentucky Star and into the woods. Beauchamp drove like he was crazy. He **gun**ned for trees and then **swerved** away from them at the last minute, **whoop**ing and hollering the whole time.

"You ain't going to believe what I got to show you," Beauchamp hollered at him.

"No, sir," said Rob weakly.

"What?" Beauchamp shouted.

"No, sir," Rob shouted back. "I ain't going to believe it."

But he did believe it. He believed it with all his heart.

chapter

19

Beauchamp hit the brakes.

"We're almost there," he said. "You got to close your eyes so it's a surprise."

Rob closed his eyes and the jeep went forward slowly. "Don't **cheat** now," Beauchamp said. "Keep them eyes closed."

"Yes, sir," Rob said.

"All right," Beauchamp said finally. "Go on and open them up."

He had **pulled** the jeep **up** as close to the tiger cage as possible without driving right into it. "Tell me what you see," he **crow**ed. "Tell me what is before your very eyes."

"A tiger," said Rob. He let his mouth drop open. He tried to look excited and **amaze**d.

"Damn straight," said Beauchamp. "King of the jungle.

And he's all mine."

"Wow," said Rob. "You own him?"

"That's right," said Beauchamp. "**Fellow** I know **owed** me some money. Paid me with a tiger. That's the way real men do business. In tigers. He come complete with the cage." The **toothpick** in the side of his mouth danced up and down; Beauchamp put a finger up to **steady** it into silence.

"What are you going to do with him?" Rob asked.

"I'm studying my options. I **figure** I could set him up out front of the Kentucky Star, have him draw me some more business into the motel."

The tiger stood and stared at Beauchamp. Beauchamp looked away from him. He **tap**ped his thick fingers on the steering wheel.★

"I also might just kill him," Beauchamp said, "and **skin** him and make me a tiger coat. I ain't made up my mind. He's a lot of work, I'll tell you that. He needs meat twice a day. That's where you come in. I need you to come out here and **feed** him. Two bucks✴ every time you do it. How's that sound?"

Rob **swallow**ed hard. "How do I get the meat in the cage?" he asked.

★ steering wheel 자동차의 핸들.
✴ buck 달러를 나타내는 속어.

74

Beauchamp **dug** in his pocket and pulled out a set of keys. "With these," he said. He shook the keys and they gave a sad **jingle**. "Don't pay no **attention** to the big keys. They're for the locks on the door. Open them up and that tiger will get out and eat you for sure. You understand? I ought not to give you this whole set, but I know you won't open up that door. Right? You ain't no fool, right?"

Rob, **terrified** that keys to the cage **exist**ed and that they were about to be handed to him, **nod**ded.

"See this tiny key?" Beauchamp said.

Rob nodded again.

"That's for the food door, right there." Beauchamp pointed at a small door at the bottom of the cage. "You just open that up and **toss** the meat in, a piece at a time. Like this."

Beauchamp **swung** himself out of the jeep with a **grunt**. He reached in the back seat for the **grocery** bag, took out a piece of meat, bent over and unlocked the tiny door, opened it and threw the meat in. The tiger **leap**ed forward, and Beauchamp took a quick step backward, **stumbling**.

"That's all there is to it," he said, **straighten**ing up. His **forehead** was shiny with **sweat**, and his hands were **trembling**.

"What's the tiger's name?" Rob asked.

"Name?" said Beauchamp. "He ain't got a name. You got to name something before you toss it a piece of meat?"

Rob **shrug**ged and **blush**ed. He bent over to scratch his legs so that he wouldn't have to look at Beauchamp's **sweaty**, angry face.

"You want to get introduced proper?" said Beauchamp in a **mock**ing voice. "Well then, get on out of the jeep."

Rob climbed down.

Beauchamp **grab**bed hold of the fence and shook it. The tiger looked up from his meat. His **muzzle** was red with blood; he stared at Beauchamp with a **fierce** look in his eyes that was familiar to Rob.

"Hey!" Beauchamp shouted. "You see this boy here?" He pointed at Rob. "He's your meal ticket. Not me. It's this boy. He's got the keys now. Understand? I don't got them no more. This boy's got them. He's your boy."

The tiger stared at Beauchamp a minute more, and then he slowly lowered his head and started back to work on the meat.

"Now you two know each other," said Beauchamp. He pulled a **tatter**ed bandanna* from his pocket and wiped the sweat off his forehead.

On the hair-raising ride back to the Kentucky Star,

★bandanna 반다나. 목이나 머리에 두르는 화려한 색상의 스카프.

Rob realized who the tiger's stare **remind**ed him of. It was Sistine. He knew that when he told her he had the keys to the cage, her eyes would **glow** with the same fierce light. He knew that she would **insist** that now they had to let the tiger go.

20

The last thing Beauchamp said to him was, "Don't forget now, this is our business deal. It don't **concern** nobody else. You take that bag of meat and hide it somewhere and I'll bring you more meat tomorrow. **In the meantime,** you keep your mouth shut."

At three o'clock, the school bus **pulled up, belch**ing and **gasping** and **sigh**ing. Norton and Billy Threemonger started **pelt**ing Rob with date palms* before the bus even came to a complete stop. The bus door opened and Sistine came running toward him, **dodging** the dates, looking as serious as a soldier on a **battlefield.**

"Let's go see the tiger," she shouted to him.

Rob was **dismayed** to see that she was still wearing his

★ date palm 대추야자. 원형 또는 긴 타원형의 열매로, 맛이 달며 영양분이 풍부하여 식량으로 이용된다.

shirt and jeans.

"Where's your dress?" he **blurt**ed.

"In here," she said. She held up the same **grocery** bag he had given her the night before. "I changed as soon as I got out of the house. My mother doesn't know. I found a book in the library today and read about big cats. Do you know that panthers✶ live in the woods here? We could **set** the tiger **free**, and he could live with them. Come on," she said. She started to run.

Rob ran, too. But the keys to the cage felt heavy in his pocket, and they **bump**ed up against his leg and slowed him down so that Sistine **beat** him there. When he arrived, she was standing **press**ed up against the fence, her fingers **wrap**ped in the chainlink.

"Tigers are an **endanger**ed **species**, you know," she said. "It's up to us to save him."

"**Watch out** he don't attack you," Rob said.

"He won't. Tigers only attack people if they're **desperate**ly hungry."

"Well, this one ain't hungry."

"How do you know?" Sistine asked, turning around and looking at him.

"Well," said Rob, "he ain't **skinny**, is he? He don't look

✶panther 아메리카 표범.

starved."

Sistine stared at him hard.

And Rob opened his mouth and let the word fall out. "*Keys*," he said. Every secret magic word he had ever known—*tiger* and *cancer* and *Caroline*—every word in his **suitcase** seemed to fall right out of him when he stood before Sistine.

"What?" she said.

"Keys," he said again. He cleared his **throat**. "I got the keys to the cage."

"How?"

"Beauchamp," he told her. "He **hire**d me to **feed** his tiger. And he gave me the keys."

"All right!" said Sistine. "Now all we have to do is open the locks and let him go."

"No," said Rob.

"Are you crazy?" she asked him.

"It ain't safe. It ain't safe for him. My friend Willie May, she had a bird and let it go, and it just got ate up."

"You're not **making sense**," she told him. "This is a tiger. A tiger, not a bird. And I don't know who Willie May is and I don't care. You can't stop me from letting this tiger go. I'll do it without the keys. I'll **saw** the locks off myself."

"Don't," said Rob.

"Don't," she **mock**ed back. And then she **spun** around

80

and grabbed hold of the cage and shook it the same way Beauchamp had earlier that day.

"I hate this place," she said. "I can't wait for my dad to come and get me. When he gets here, I'm going to make him come out here and set this tiger free. That's the first thing we'll do." She shook the cage harder. "I'll get you out of here," she said to the **pacing** tiger. "I promise." She **rattle**d the cage as if she were the one who was locked up. The tiger paced back and forth without stopping.

"Don't," said Rob.

But she didn't stop. She shook the cage and beat her head against the chainlink, and then he heard her gasp. He was afraid that maybe she was **choking**. He went and stood next to her. And he saw that she was crying. *Crying.* Sistine.

He stood beside her, **terrified** and amazed. When his mother was alive—when he still cried about things—she had been the one who **comfort**ed him. She would **cup** her hand around the back of his neck and say to him, "You go on and cry. I got you. I got good hold of you."

Before Rob could think whether it was right or whether it was wrong, he reached out and put his **palm** on Sistine's neck. He could feel her **pulse**, beating **in time** with the tiger's pacing. He **whisper**ed to her the same words his mother had whispered to him. "I got you," he told her. "I got good hold of you."

Sistine cried and cried. She cried as if she would never stop. And she did not tell him to take his hand away.

21

By the time they started walking back to the Kentucky Star, it was **dusk**. Sistine was not crying, but she wasn't talking either, not even about letting the tiger go.

"I have to call my mother," she said to him in a tired voice when they got to the motel.

"I'll go with you," said Rob.

She didn't tell him not to, so he walked with her across the **parking lot**. They were almost to the **laundry** room when Willie May **materialize**d out of the purple darkness. She was **lean**ing up against her car, smoking a **cigarette**.

"Boo,*" she said to Rob.

"Hey," he told her back.

"Somebody following you," she said, **jerk**ing her head at

★boo 어이! 사람을 놀라게 하거나 겁을 주려고 할 때 외치는 소리.

Sistine.

"This is Sistine," Rob told her. And then he turned to Sistine and said, "This is Willie May, the one I was telling you about, the one who had the bird and let it go."

"So what?" said Sistine.

"So nothing," said Willie May. Her glasses **wink**ed in the light from the falling Kentucky Star. "So I had me a bird."

"Why are you **hang**ing **around** in the parking lot trying to **scare** people?" Sistine asked, her voice hard and **mean**.

"I ain't trying to scare people," said Willie May.

"Willie May works here," said Rob.

"That's right," said Willie May. She reached into the front pocket of her dress and pulled out a package of Eight Ball gum. "You know what?" she said to Sistine. "I know you. You ain't got to introduce yourself to me. You angry. You got all the anger in the world inside you. I know angry when I meet it. Been angry most of my life."

"I'm not angry," Sistine **snap**ped.

"All right," said Willie May. She opened the package of Eight Ball. "You an angry liar, then. Here you go." She held out a **stick** of gum to Sistine.

Sistine **stare**d for a long minute at Willie May, and Willie May stared back. The last light of dusk disappeared and the darkness moved in. Rob held his breath. He wanted **desperate**ly for the two of them to like each other. When Sistine finally reached out and took the gum from Willie May, he let his breath go in a quiet *whoosh*.✶

Willie May **nodd**ed at Sistine, and then she **extend**ed the pack to Rob. He took a piece and put it in his pocket for later.

Willie May **lit** another cigarette and laughed. "Ain't that just like God," she said, "throwing the two of you together?" She shook her head. "This boy full of **sorrow**, keeping it down low in his legs. And you,"—she pointed her cigarette at Sistine—"you all full of anger, got it snapping out of you like **lightning**. You some **pair**, that's the truth." She put her arms over her head and **stretch**ed and then **straighten**ed up and stepped away from the car.

Sistine stared at Willie May, with her mouth open. "How tall are you?" she asked.

"Six feet✶ two," said Willie May. "And I got to get on home. But first, I got some advice for you. I already gave this boy some advice. You ready for yours?"

Sistine nodded, her mouth still open.

"This is it: Ain't nobody going to come and **rescue**

✶ whoosh 쉿 하는 소리.
✶ feet 길이의 단위 피트. 1피트는 약 30.48센티미터이다. six feet two는 6피트 2인치를 말하며 약 187cm이다.

you," said Willie May. She opened the car door and sat down behind the wheel. "You got to rescue yourself. You understand what I mean?"

Sistine stared at Willie May. She said nothing.

Willie May **crank**ed the engine. Rob and Sistine watched her drive away.

"I think she's a **prophetess**," said Sistine.

"A what?" Rob said.

"A prophetess," said Sistine. "They're painted all over the Sistine **ceiling**. They're women who God speaks through."

"Oh," said Rob, "a prophetess." He turned the word over in his mouth. "Prophetess," he said again. He nodded. That sounded right. If God was going to talk through somebody, it **made sense** to Rob that he would pick Willie May.

chapter

22

"You out in the woods with that girl again?" his father asked as soon as Rob stepped into the room.

"Yes, sir," said Rob.

"Look over here, son." His father was standing by Rob's bed.

"Sir?" said Rob. His heart **sank**. He knew what his father had found: the meat. He had hidden it under his bed until it was time to go and **feed** the tiger again.

"Where'd this meat come from?" his father asked, pointing at the bloody brown bag.

Without thinking, Rob said, "Beauchamp."

"Beauchamp," his father repeated, low and dark. "Beauchamp. He don't **hardly** pay me enough to **get by**, and now he's giving us his **rot**ten meat. He thinks I ain't man enough to put meat on my own table."

Rob wanted to say something, but then he thought of Beauchamp and **held his tongue.**

"I ought to teach him a lesson," his father said. The cords* in his neck stood out like **twig**s. He kicked the bag of meat. "I ought to," he said. "Making me work for less than nothing, giving us rotten meat."

He went and stood in front of the gun case. He didn't unlock it. He just stood and stared and **crack**ed his **knuckle**s.

"Daddy," said Rob. But he couldn't think of anything to say after that. His mother had known how to calm his father. She would put her hand on his arm or say his name in a soft and **reproachful** voice, and that would be enough. But Rob didn't know how to do those things. He stood for a minute more, and then he walked over to his bed and **grab**bed a piece of wood and his knife. As he left the room, his father was still standing at the locked gun case, staring through the glass at the deer-hunting **rifle**, as if he was trying to **will** the gun into his hands.

Rob walked to the Kentucky Star sign. He sat down underneath it and leaned up against one of the cold, **damp pole**s and started to work on the wood.

But his head was too full of his father's anger and

★cords (= vocal cords) 성대(聲帶).

Sistine's tears. He couldn't **concentrate**. He looked up at the dark underside of the sign and **recall**ed **lying** on a **blanket**, staring up at a big oak tree.* His mother had been on one side of him, and his father, asleep and **snoring**, had been on the other. He remembered that his mother had taken hold of his hand and pointed up at the sun shining through the leaves of the tree and said, "Look, Rob, I have never in my life seen a prettier color of green. Ain't it perfect?"

"Yes, ma'am," he said, staring at the trees. "It looks like the original green. The first one God ever thought up."

His mother **squeeze**d his hand hard. "That's right," she said. "The first one God ever thought up. The **first-ever** green. You and me, we see the world the same."

He concentrated on that green. He let it **seep** through a crack in his **suitcase** of not-thoughts and fill up his head with color. He wondered if Willie May's Cricket had been the same bright and original green. That's what he thought about as he **carved**. And so he wasn't surprised, when he stopped and held the wood away from himself, to see a wing and a **beak** and a tiny eye. It was Cricket, Willie May's Cricket, coming to life under his knife.

He worked on the bird for a long time, until it looked

★ oak tree 참나무.

so real that he half expected it to **break into** song. When he finally went back to the room, he found his father asleep in the **recliner**. The gun case was still locked, and the bag of meat was gone. He wouldn't be able to feed the tiger in the morning. He would have to wait until Beauchamp brought him another package.

Rob went and stood over his father and stared down at him. He looked at his heavy hands and the **bald spot** on his nodding head. He was memorizing him and trying at the same time to understand him, to **make** some **sense** out of him, out of his anger and his quiet, **comparing** it to the way he used to sing and smile, when his father **jerk**ed awake.

"Hey," he said.

"Hey," Rob said back.

"What time is it?"

"I ain't sure," said Rob. "Late, I guess."

His father **sigh**ed. "Go on and get me that leg medicine."

Rob brought him the tube of medicine.

Outside the motel room, the world **creak**ed and sighed. The rain started in again, and his father's hands were gentle as he **applied** the **ointment** to Rob's legs.

23

The next morning, Rob put the keys to the tiger cage in one pocket and the wooden bird in the other, and set out looking for Willie May.

He found her in the **laundry** room, sitting on one of the **foldup** chairs, smoking a **cigarette** and staring into space.

"Hey there," she said to him. "Where's your lady friend at?"

"School," said Rob. "But today's only a half day.*" He kept his hands in his pockets. Now that he stood before Willie May, he was afraid to give her the bird. What if it was wrong? What if he had carved it wrong and it didn't look anything like the real Cricket?

★ half day 반나절만 수업 혹은 근무하는 날.

"What you giving me them **shifty**-eyed looks for?" Willie May asked.

"I made you something," said Rob quickly, before he lost his **nerve**.

"Made me something?" said Willie May. "For real?"

"Uh-huh. Close your eyes and hold out your hand."

"I ain't," said Willie May. But she smiled and closed her eyes and put out her **enormous** hand, **palm** up. Rob carefully placed the bird in it.

"You can look now," he told her.

She closed her fingers around the little piece of wood, but she didn't open her eyes. She **puff**ed on her cigarette; the long gray **ash** on the end of it **trembled**.

"Don't need to look," she finally said. The cigarette ash dropped to the floor. "I know what I got in my hand. It's Cricket."

"But you got to look at it and tell me did I do it right," said Rob.

"I ain't got to do nothing," said Willie May, "except stay black and die." She opened her eyes slowly, as if she was afraid she might **frighten** the bird into flying away. "This the right bird," she said, nodding her head, "this the one."

"Now you don't got to dream about him no more," said Rob.

"That's right," said Willie May. "Where'd you learn to work a piece of wood like this?"

"My mama," said Rob.

Willie May nodded. "She taught you good."

"Yes, ma'am," said Rob. He stared down at his legs. "I know a wooden bird ain't the same as having a real one."

"It ain't," agreed Willie May. "But it **soothe**s my heart just the same."

"My dad said he ain't got no jobs for me until this afternoon. He said I could help you out this morning."

"Well," said Willie May. She dropped the bird into the front pocket of her dress. "I might could find some way for you to help me."

So Rob spent his morning following Willie May from room to room, **strip**ping the dirty sheets from the beds. And while he worked, the keys **jingle**d in his pocket, and he knew that soon Sistine would be out of school and that she would **demand** again that he unlock the cage and let the tiger go.

chapter

24

"Where's the **prophetess**?" Sistine asked him as soon as she stepped off the bus. She was wearing a bright orange dress with pink circles all over it. Her left knee was **skin**ned and **bleed**ing, and her right eye was **swollen.**

"Huh?" said Rob. He stood and stared at her and wondered how she could get into so many fights in only half a day of school.

"Willie May," said Sistine. "Where is she?"

"She's **vacuum**ing," said Rob.

Sistine started walking **purposeful**ly toward the Kentucky Star. She talked to Rob without looking back. "My mother found out that I was wearing your clothes to school," she said. "She took them away from me. I'm in trouble. I'm not supposed to come out here any more."

"You know," said Rob, "you don't always got to get in

94

fights. Sometimes, if you don't hit them back, they leave you alone."

She **whirl**ed around and **faced** him. "I want to get in fights," she said fiercely. "I want to hit them back. Sometimes I hit them first."

"Oh," said Rob.

Sistine turned back around. "I'm going to find the prophetess," she said loudly. "I'm going to ask her what we should do about the tiger."

"You can't ask her about the tiger," said Rob. "Beauchamp said I ain't supposed to tell nobody, especially not Willie May."

Sistine didn't answer him; she started to run. And Rob, to **keep up** with her, ran too.

They found Willie May vacuuming the **shag** carpet in room 203. Sistine went up behind her and **tap**ped her on the back. Willie May whirled around with her **fist clench**ed, like a boxer.*

"We need some answers," Sistine shouted over the **roar** of the vacuum cleaner.

Willie May **bent** down and turned the vacuum cleaner off.

"Well," she said, "look who's here." She kept her hand

★ boxer 복서. 프로 권투 선수.

balled up, as if she was still searching for something to hit.

"What's in your hand?" Sistine asked.

Willie May **uncurl**ed her fist and showed Sistine the bird.

"Oh," said Sistine. And Rob realized then why he liked Sistine so much. He liked her because when she saw something beautiful, the sound of her voice changed. All the words she **utter**ed had an *oof* sound to them, as if she was getting **punch**ed in the stomach. The sound was in her voice when she talked about the Sistine Chapel and when she looked at the things he carved in wood. It was there when she said the **poem** about the tiger burning bright and it was there when she talked about Willie May being a prophetess. Her words sounded the way all those things made him feel, as if the world, the real world, had been punched through, so that he could see something wonderful and **dazzling** on the other side of it.

"Did Rob make it?" Sistine asked Willie May.

"He did," said Willie May.

"It looks alive. Is it like your bird that you let go?"

"Just about exactly," said Willie May.

"I . . . ," said Sistine. She looked at Willie May. Then she turned and looked at Rob. "We," she said, "We need to ask you something."

"Ask on," said Willie May.

"If you knew about something that was locked up in a cage, something big and beautiful that was locked away un**fair**ly, for no good reason, and you had the keys to the cage, would you let it go?"

Willie May sat down on the bed. A cloud of **dust** rose up around her. "Lord God,★" she said. "What you two children got in a cage?"

"It's a tiger," Rob said. He felt like he had to be the one who said it. He was the one who found the tiger. He was the one who had the keys to the cage.

"A what?" said Willie May.

"A tiger," said Sistine.

"Do Jesus!✲" **exclaim**ed Willie May.

"It's true," said Sistine.

Willie May shook her head. She looked up at the ceiling. She let out her breath in a loud slow **hiss** of **disapproval**. "All right," she said. "Why don't you all show me where you got this tiger locked up in a cage?"

★ Lord God [감탄사] 어이쿠, 저런!
✲ Do Jesus [감탄사] 어머나, 저런!

chapter

25

The three of them walked through the woods in silence. Sistine and Rob chewed Eight Ball gum, and Willie May smoked a cigarette, and nobody said a word.

"Lord God," said Willie May when they came up to the cage. She stared at the pacing animal. "Ain't no reason to doubt the fierceness of God when He make something like that," she said. "Who was the fool that caged this tiger up?"

"He belongs to Beauchamp," Rob told her.

"Beauchamp," said Willie May with disgust. She shook her head. "One person in the world that don't need to be owning no tiger, and that's Beauchamp."

"See?" said Sistine. "It's not right, is it? Just like you told Rob about your bird and how you had to let it go."

"A bird," said Willie May, "that's one thing. Tiger

belonging to Beauchamp is another."

"Tell Rob that he should unlock the cage and let him go," Sistine **demand**ed.

"I ain't," said Willie May. "You got to ask yourself what's going to happen to this tiger after you let him go. How's he going to live?"

Rob was **flood**ed with sad **relief**. Willie May wasn't going to make him do it. He wasn't going to lose the tiger.

"Panthers live in these woods," **argue**d Sistine. "They survive."

"Used to," said Willie May. "Don't no more."

Sistine put her hands on her hips. "You're not saying what you believe," she **accuse**d. "You're not talking like a **prophetess**."

"That's 'cause I ain't no prophetess," said Willie May. "All I am is somebody speaking the truth. And the truth is: there ain't nothing you can do for this tiger except to let it be."

"It's not right," said Sistine.

"Right ain't got nothing to do with it," **mutter**ed Willie May. "Sometimes right don't **count**."

"I can't wait until my father comes to get me," said Sistine. "He knows what's right. He'll **set** this tiger **free**."

Rob looked at Sistine. "Your daddy ain't coming for you," he said softly, shaking his head, **amaze**d at what he suddenly knew to be the truth.

"My father is coming to get me," Sistine said through tight lips.

"Naw," said Rob sadly. "He ain't. He's a liar. Like your mama said."

"You're the liar," said Sistine in a dark cold voice. Her face was so white that it seemed to **glow** before him. "And I hate you," she said to him. "Everybody at school hates you, too. Even the teachers. You are a sissy.★ I hope I never ever see you again."

She turned and walked away, and Rob stood and **consider**ed her words. He felt them on his skin like **shard**s of broken glass. He was afraid to move. He was afraid of how deep they might go inside him.

"She don't mean it," said Willie May. "She don't mean none of what she say right now."

Rob **shrug**ged. He bent and **scratch**ed his legs as hard as he could. He scratched and scratched, **dig**ging his nails in deep, trying to get to the bottom of the **itch** that was always there.

"Stop it," Willie May told him.

Rob looked up at her.

"Let me tell you something," she said. "I would love

★ sissy 여자 같은 남자.

100

to see this tiger rise on up out of this cage. Yes, uh-huh. I would like to see him rise on up and attack Beauchamp; **serve** him right for keeping a wild animal locked up, putting you in the middle of this, giving you the keys to this cage. Come on." She **grab**bed hold of Rob's hand. "Let's get on up out of here."

As they walked back to the Kentucky Star, Rob thought about what Willie May had said about the tiger rising on up. It **remind**ed him of what she had said about his sadness needing to rise up. And when he thought about the two things together, the tiger and his sadness, the truth circled over and above him and then came and landed lightly on his shoulder. He knew what he had to do.

26

He left Willie May at the motel and went down the **highway**.

"Sistine!" he shouted as he ran. "Sistine!" he screamed.

And **miraculous**ly he saw her—her orange dress with the pink polka dots*—**glow**ing on the **horizon**. Sistine Bailey.

"Hey," he shouted. "Sistine. I got something to tell you."

"I'm not talking to you," she shouted back. But she stopped. She turned around. She put her hands on her hips.

He ran faster.

"I come to tell you about the tiger," he said when he

★ polka dot 물방울 무늬.

caught up with her.

"What about him?"

"I'm fixing to let him go," said Rob.

Sistine **squint**ed her eyes at him. "You won't do it," she said.

"Yes, I will," he told her. He reached into his pocket and pulled out the keys and held them in front of her proudly, as if he had just **conjure**d them out of thin air, as if they had never **exist**ed before. "I'm going to do it," he said. "I'm going to do it for you."

"Whoooooeeee!!!!!" somebody screamed, and Rob turned and saw Beauchamp come speeding right toward them in his red jeep.

"Oh no," **whisper**ed Rob.

"Is it him?" Sistine whispered.

Rob **nod**ded.

Beauchamp **pull**ed **over** to the side of the road, spraying mud and water everywhere.

"You out getting your exercise?" he **holler**ed.

Rob **shrug**ged.

"Speak up," **roar**ed Beauchamp. He got out of the jeep and came toward them. Rob quickly **pocket**ed the keys. His heart **thump**ed once, loudly, as if it was **caution**ing him to keep quiet, and then it went back to **beat**ing normally.

"Well, looky here," said Beauchamp when he saw Sistine. "You out **chasing** girls. Is that it? Man after my own heart. This your girlfriend?" Beauchamp **pound**ed Rob on the back.

"No, sir," said Rob. He looked at Sistine. She was staring so hard at Beauchamp that Rob was afraid the man might **burst into flames.**

"I got more goods for you," Beauchamp said. "I left 'em back at the motel with Ida Belle."

"Yes, sir," said Rob.

"What's your name, little thing?" Beauchamp said, turning to Sistine.

Rob's heart gave another warning thump. Lord only knew what Sistine would say to Beauchamp.

But Sistine, as always, surprised him. She smiled sweetly at Beauchamp. "Sissy," she said.

"Well, that's pretty," said Beauchamp. "That's the kind of name **worth** running down the road after." He **lean**ed over to Rob. "Remember what we got going. You're keeping your **manly** secrets, ain't you?"

"Yes, sir," said Rob.

Beauchamp **wink**ed. His **toothpick wiggle**d.

"I got me some business in town," he said. He **squeeze**d Rob's shoulder hard and then took his hand away. "You and your girlfriend stay out of trouble now, you hear?"

"Yes, sir," said Rob.

Beauchamp **swagger**ed back to the jeep, and Rob and Sistine stood together and watched him get in it and roar down the highway.

"He's afraid," said Sistine. "He's afraid of the tiger. That's why he's making you **feed** him."

Rob nodded. That was another truth he had known without knowing it, the same as he had known that Sistine's father was not coming back. He must, he realized, know somewhere, deep inside him, more things than he had ever dreamed of.

"I'm sorry," he said. "What I said about your daddy, I'm sorry."

"I don't want to talk about my father," said Sistine.

"Maybe he *is* coming to get you."

"He's not coming to get me." Sistine **toss**ed her head. "And I don't care. It doesn't **matter**. What matters is the tiger. Let's go. Let's go **set** him **free**."

27

The first key **slid** into the first lock so **smooth**ly that it made Rob **dizzy** with **amaze**ment. It was going to be so easy to let the tiger go.

"Hurry," Sistine said to him. "Hurry up. Get the other locks."

He opened the second lock and the third. And then he took them off one by one and handed them to Sistine, who laid them on the ground.

"Now open the door," she said.

Rob's heart **pound**ed and **flutter**ed in his chest. "What if he eats us?" he asked.

"He won't," said Sistine. "He'll leave us alone out of **gratitude**. We're his **emancipators**."

Rob **flung** the door wide.

"Get out of the way," he shouted, and they both

jumped back from the door and waited. But the tiger **ignore**d them. He continued to **pace** back and forth in the cage, **oblivious** to the open door.

"Go on," Rob said to him.

"You're free," Sistine whispered.

But the tiger did not even look in the direction of the door.

Sistine **crept** forward and **grab**bed hold of the cage. She shook it.

"Get out!" she screamed. "Come on," she said, turning to Rob, "help me. Help me get him out."

Rob grabbed hold of the fence and shook it. "Get," he said.

The tiger stopped pacing and turned to stare at them both **cling**ing like monkeys to the cage.

"Go on!" Rob shouted, suddenly **furious**. He shook the cage harder. He **yell**ed. He put his head back and **howl**ed, and he saw that the sky above them was thick with clouds, and that made him even angrier. He yelled louder; he shouted at the dark sky. He shook the cage as hard as he could.

Sistine put a hand on his arm. "Shhh," she said. "He's leaving. Watch."

As they stared, the tiger stepped with **grace** and **delicacy** out of the cage. He put his nose up and **sniff**ed.

He took one tiny step and then another. Then he stopped and stood **still**. Sistine **clap**ped her hands, and the tiger turned and looked back at them both, his eyes **blazing**. And then he started to run.

He ran so fast, it looked to Rob like he was flying. His muscles moved like a river; it was hard to believe that a cage had ever **contain**ed him. It didn't seem possible.

The tiger went **leap**ing through the grass, moving **farther** and farther away from Rob and Sistine. He looked like the sun, rising and **set**ting again and again. And watching him go, Rob felt his own heart rising and falling, beating **in time**.

chapter

28

"Oh," said Sistine, in that voice that Rob loved. "See," she said, "that was the right thing. That was the right thing to do."

Rob nodded. But in his mind he saw a **flash** of green. He remembered what happened to Cricket.

"What?" said Sistine, turning to him. "What are you thinking about?"

Rob shook his head. "Nothing," he told her.

"*Roberrttt.*" The sound of his name came **float**ing to them from the direction of the motel.

"That's my dad," he said, **confus**ed. "That's my dad calling me."

And then they heard Willie May. "Do Jesus!" she screamed, her voice high and wild.

And then there was the **crack** of a gun.

They both stood **still, stun**ned and silent. And when Willie May came running out from under the pine trees and saw them, she stopped. "Thank you, Jesus," she said, looking up at the sky. "Two **whole** children. Thank you. Come here," she said. She opened her arms. "Come to me."

Rob started walking toward her. He wanted to tell her that she was wrong. He wanted to tell her that he did not feel whole. But he did not have the energy or the heart to say anything; all he could manage was to put one foot in front of the other. All he could do was keep walking toward Willie May.

Willie May led them back. And when Rob saw the tiger on the ground and his father standing over it, holding the **rifle**, he felt something rise up in him, an anger as big and powerful as the tiger. Bigger.

"You killed him," he said to his father.

"I had to," his father said.

"That was my tiger!" Rob screamed. "You killed him! You killed my tiger!" He ran at his father and attacked him. He **beat** him with his **fist**s. He kicked him. But his father stood like a wall. He held the gun up over his head and kept his eyes open and took each hit without **blink**ing.

And Rob saw that hitting wasn't going to be enough. So he did something he thought he would never do. He opened his **suitcase**. And the words **sprang** out of it, **coil**ed and **explosive**.

"I wish it had been you!" he screamed. "I wish it had been you that died! I hate you! You ain't the one I need. I need her! I need her!"

The world, and everything in it, seemed to stop moving.

He stared at his father.

His father stared at him.

"Say her name!" Rob screamed into the silence. "You say it!"

"Caroline," his father **whisper**ed, with the gun still over his head, with his eyes still open.

And with that word, with the small sound of his mother's name, the world **lurch**ed back into **motion**; like an old merry-go-round,* it started to **spin** again. His father put the gun down and pulled Rob to him.

"Caroline," his father whispered. "Caroline, Caroline, Caroline."

Rob **buried** his face in his father's shirt. It smelled like **sweat** and turpentine* and green leaves. "I need her," Rob said.

"I need her, too," said his father, pulling Rob closer.

✶ merry-go-round 회전목마.
✶ turpentine 테레빈유(油). 페인트를 희석하는 데 사용한다.

"But we don't got her. Neither one of us. What we got, all we got, is each other. And we got to learn to make do with that."

"I ain't going to cry," Rob said, shutting his eyes, but the tears leaked out of him anyway. Then they came in a rush and he couldn't stop. He cried from somewhere deep inside of himself, from the place where his mother had been, the same place that the tiger had been and was gone from now.

Rob looked up and saw his father wiping tears from his own eyes.

"All right," said his father, holding Rob tight. "That's all right," he said. "You're okay."

When Rob finally looked up again, he saw Willie May holding Sistine like she was a baby, rocking her and saying *shhh*.

Willie May stared back at him. "Don't think you gonna start pounding on me now," she said.

"No, ma'am," said Rob. He wiped the back of his hand across his nose and slid out of his father's arms.

"I went and got your daddy," Willie May told Rob as she swayed back and forth, rocking Sistine. "I figured out what you was gonna do. And there ain't no telling what that tiger would've done once he got out of that cage. I went and got your daddy, so he could save you."

"Yes, ma'am," said Rob.

He went and stood over the open-eyed tiger. The **bullet** hole in his head was red and small; it didn't look big enough to kill him.

"Go ahead and touch him," said Sistine.

Rob looked up. She was standing beside him. Her dress was **twist**ed and **wrinkle**d. Her eyes were red. Rob stared at her and she nodded. So he **knelt** and put out a hand and placed it on the tiger's head. He felt the tears rise up in him again.

Sistine **crouch**ed down next to him. She put her hand on the tiger, too. "He was so pretty," she said. "He was one of the prettiest things I have ever seen."

Rob nodded.

"We have to have a **funeral** for him," Sistine said. "He's a **fallen warrior**. We have to bury him right."

Rob sat down next to the tiger and ran his hand over the rough **fur** again and again while the tears traveled down his cheeks and dropped onto the ground.

chapter

29

Rob and his father worked with **shovels** to **dig** a hole that was deep enough and wide enough and dark enough to hold the tiger. And the whole time, it rained.

"We got to say some words over him," said Willie May when the hole was done and the tiger was in it. "Can't cover up nothing without saying some words."

"I'll say the **poem**," said Sistine. She folded her hands in front of her and looked down at the ground. "'Tiger, tiger, burning bright / in the forests of the night,'" she **recited**.

Rob closed his eyes.

"'What **immortal** hand or eye / Could **frame** thy* fearful symmetry?'" Sistine continued. "'In what **distant** deeps or skies / Burnt the fire of thine* eyes? / On what

---

★ thy your의 고어. 당신의.
✳ thine yours의 고어. 당신의 것.

wings **dare** he **aspire?**'"

To Rob, the words sounded like music, but better. His eyes filled up with tears again. He worried that now that he had started crying, he might never stop.

"That's all I remember," Sistine said after a minute. "There's more to it, but I can't remember it all. You say something now, Rob," she said.

"I don't got nothing to say," said Rob, "except for, I loved him."

"Well," said Willie May. "What I got to say is I ain't had good experiences with animals in cages." She reached into her dress pocket and took out the wooden bird and **bent** down and **laid** it on top of the tiger. "That ain't nothing," she said to the tiger, "just a little bird to keep you **company.**" She stepped back, away from the **grave.**

Rob's father cleared his **throat.** He **hum**med softly, and Rob thought he was going to sing, but instead he shook his head and said, "I had to shoot him. I'm sorry, but I had to shoot him. For Rob."

Rob **lean**ed into his father, and it felt for a minute like his father leaned back. Then Rob picked up his shovel and started covering the tiger with dirt. As he filled the grave, something danced and **flicker**ed on his arm. Rob **stare**d at it, wondering what it was. And then he **recognize**d it. It was the sun. Showing up **in time** for another **funeral.**

"I'm sorry I made you do it," Sistine said to Rob when he was done. "He wouldn't be dead if I hadn't made you do it."

"It's all right," Rob said. "I ain't sorry about what I did."

"We can make a **headstone** for him," said Sistine. "And we can bring flowers and put them on his grave—fresh ones, every day." She **slip**ped her hand into his. "I didn't mean what I said before, about you being a sissy. And I don't hate you. You're my best friend."

The whole way back to the Kentucky Star, Rob held on to Sistine's hand. He **marvel**ed at what a small hand it was and how much **comfort** there was in holding on to it.

And he marveled, too, at how different he felt inside, how much lighter, as if he had set something heavy down and walked away from it, without **bother**ing to look back.

chapter

30

That night, his father sang to Rob as he put the medicine on his legs. He sang the song about **mining** for gold, the one that he used to sing with Rob's mother. When he was done with the medicine and the song, he cleared his **throat** and said, "Caroline loved that song."

"Me too," Rob told him. "I like it too."

His father stood up. "You're going to have to tell Beauchamp that you was the one that let that tiger go."

"Yes, sir," said Rob.

"I'll tell him I was the one who shot him, but you got to admit to letting him go."

"Yes, sir," said Rob again.

"I might could lose my job over it," his father said.

"I know it," Rob told him. But he wasn't afraid. He thought about Beauchamp's shaking hands. Beauchamp was the **coward**. He knew that now. "I thought I would tell him I could work for him to pay for what I done."

"You can **offer** him up some **reasonable** kind of solution," said his father, "but it don't mean he'll go for it. There ain't no **predict**ing Beauchamp. Other than to say he's going to be mad."

Rob **nod**ded.

"And on Monday," his father continued, "I **aim** to call that **principal** and tell him you're going back to school. I ain't **mess**ing **around** with taking you to more doctors. You're going back and that's that."

"Yes, sir," said Rob. He didn't **mind** the thought of going back to school. School was where Sistine would be.

His father cleared his throat. "It's hard for me to talk about your mama. I wouldn't never have believed that I could miss somebody the way I miss her. Saying her name pains me." He **bent** his head and **concentrate**d on putting the cap on the tube of medicine. "But I'll say it for you," he said. "I'll try **on account of** you."

Rob looked at his father's hands. They were the hands that had held the gun that shot the tiger. They were the hands that put the medicine on his legs. They were the hands that had held him when he cried. They were **complicate**d hands, Rob thought.

"You want some macaroni and cheese for dinner?" his

father asked, looking back up at Rob.

"That sounds all right," said Rob. "Macaroni and cheese sounds real good."

That night, Rob dreamed he and Sistine were standing at the **grave** of the tiger. They were watching and waiting. He didn't know for what. But then he saw a **flutter** of green wings and he understood. It was the wooden bird, only he wasn't made of wood, he was real. And he flew up out of the tiger's grave, and they **chase**d him, laughing and **bump**ing into each other. They tried to catch him. But they couldn't. The bird flew higher and higher until he disappeared into a sky that looked just like the Sistine **ceiling**. In his dream, Rob stood and **stare**d up at the sky, **admiring** all the **figure**s and the colors, watching as the bird disappeared into them.

"See?" said Sistine in his dream. "I told you it was like **fireworks**."

He woke up smiling, staring at the ceiling of the motel room.

"Guess what?" his father called to him from outside.

"What?" said Rob back.

"There ain't a cloud in the sky," said his father, "that's what."

Rob nodded. He **lay** in bed and watched the sun **poke**

its way through his curtain. He thought about Sistine and the tiger he wanted to make for her. He thought about what kind of wood he would use and how big he would make the tiger. He thought about how happy Sistine would be when she saw it.

He lay in bed and **consider**ed the future, and outside his window, the tiny neon Kentucky Star rose and fell and rose and fell, **competing** bravely with the light of the morning sun.

THE TIGER RISING

THE TIGER RISING

Kate DiCamillo

WORKBOOK

Contents

'아동 도서계의 노벨상!' 미국 최고 권위의 아동 문학상

뉴베리 상(Newbery Award)은 미국 도서관 협회에서 해마다 미국 아동 문학 발전에 가장 크게 이바지한 작가에게 수여하는 아동 문학상입니다. 1922년에 시작된 이 상은 미국에서 가장 오랜 역사를 지닌 아동 문학상이자, '아동 도서계의 노벨상'이라 불릴 만큼 높은 권위를 자랑하는 상입니다.

뉴베리 상은 그 역사와 권위만큼이나 심사 기준이 까다롭기로 유명한데, 심사단은 책의 주제 의식은 물론 정보의 깊이와 스토리의 정교함, 캐릭터와 문체의 적정성 등을 꼼꼼히 평가하여 수상작을 결정합니다.

그해 최고의 작품으로 선정된 도서에게는 '뉴베리 메달(Newbery Medal)'이라고 부르는 금색 메달을 수여하며, 최종 후보에 올랐던 주목할 만한 작품들에게는 '뉴베리 아너(Newbery Honor)'라는 이름의 은색 마크를 수여합니다.

뉴베리 상을 받은 도서는 미국의 모든 도서관에 비치되어 더 많은 독자들을 만나게 되며, 대부분 수십에서 수백만 부가 판매되는 베스트셀러가 됩니다. 뉴베리 상을 수상한 작가는 그만큼 필력과 작품성을 인정받게 되어, 수상 작가의 다른 작품들 또한 수상작 못지않게 커다란 주목과 사랑을 받습니다.

왜 뉴베리 수상작인가?
쉬운 어휘로 쓰인 '검증된' 영어원서!

뉴베리 수상작들은 '검증된 원서'로 국내 영어 학습자들에게 큰 사랑을 받고 있습니다. 뉴베리 수상작이 원서 읽기에 좋은 교재인 이유는 무엇일까요?

1. 아동 문학인 만큼 어휘가 어렵지 않습니다.
2. 어렵지 않은 어휘를 사용하면서도 '문학상'을 수상한 만큼 문장의 깊이가 상당합니다.
3. 적당한 난이도의 어휘와 깊이 있는 문장으로 구성되어 있기 때문에 초등 고학년부터 성인까지, 영어 초보자부터 실력자까지 모든 영어 학습자들이 읽기에 좋습니다.

실제로 뉴베리 수상작은 국제중·특목고에서는 입시 필독서로, 대학교에서는 영어 강독 교재로 다양하고 폭넓게 활용되고 있습니다. 이런 이유로 뉴베리 수상작은 한국어 번역서보다 오히려 원서가 훨씬 많이 판매되는 기현상을 보이고 있습니다.

'베스트 오브 베스트'만을 엄선한 「뉴베리 컬렉션」

「뉴베리 컬렉션」은 뉴베리 메달 및 아너 수상작, 그리고 뉴베리 수상 작가의 유명 작품들을 엄선하여 한국 영어 학습자들을 위한 최적의 교재로 재탄생시킨 영어 원서 시리즈입니다.

1. 어휘 수준과 문장의 난이도, 분량 등 국내 영어 학습자들에게 적합한 정도를 종합적으로 검토하여 선정하였습니다.
2. 기존 원서 독자층 사이의 인기도까지 감안하여 최적의 작품들을 선별하였습니다.
3. 판형이 좁고 글씨가 작아 읽기 힘들었던 원서 디자인을 대폭 수정하여, 판형을 시원하게 키우고 읽기에 최적화된 영문 서체를 사용하여 가독성을 극대화하였습니다.
4. 함께 제공되는 워크북은 어려운 어휘를 완벽하게 정리하고 이해력을 점검하는 퀴즈를 덧붙여 독자들이 원서를 보다 쉽고 재미있게 읽을 수 있도록 구성하였습니다.
5. 기존에 높은 가격에 판매되어 구입이 부담스러웠던 오디오북을 부록으로 제공하여 리스닝과 소리 내어 읽기에까지 원서를 두루 활용할 수 있도록 했습니다.

케이트 디카밀로(Kate DiCamillo)는 화려한 수상 경력을 가지고 있는, 미국의 대표적인 아동 문학 작가입니다. 그녀는 「Because of Winn-Dixie」로 뉴베리 아너를 수상하여 이름을 알리기 시작했고, 「The Tiger Rising」으로 전미도서상(National Book Award)의 최종 후보에 올랐습니다. 그리고 판타지 문학 작품인 「The Tale of Despereaux」는 "미국 아동 문학에 가장 크게 기여한" 작품이라는 평과 함께 뉴베리 메달을 수상하여 큰 인기몰이를 하였습니다. 또한 「The Miraculous Journey of Edward Tulane」으로 우수한 아동 문학에 수여하는 보스턴 글로브-혼 도서상(Boston Globe-Horn Book Award)을 받는 등 문학성을 여러 차례 검증 받고 있습니다.

「The Tiger Rising」은 가슴속 깊이 슬픔을 묻어둔 소년 롭(Rob)의 이야기를 담고 있습니다. 롭은 병으로 세상을 떠난 엄마를 땅에 묻고 그 슬픔으로 한참을 웁니다. 그러나 울어도 엄마는 돌아오지 않는다는 단호한 아빠의 말에 따라 엄마와의 추억을 마음속에 숨기고 그의 모든 감정들, 모든 희망들도 마음속 가방 안에 넣고 꺼내지 않습니다.

어느 날, 롭은 그가 거주하고 있는 모텔 뒤 숲에서 우리에 갇힌 호랑이를 보게 됩니다. 그리고 학교에 가는 버스 안에서 롭은 타지에서 전학 온 소녀 시스틴(Sistine)을 만납니다. 신기하게도 롭은 시스틴과 있기만 하면 닫아두었던 마음속 가방을 열고 숨겨둔 이야기를 하게 됩니다. 시스틴 역시 롭에게 자기 부모님에 대한 불만을 털어 놓으며 조금씩 마음을 엽니다.

롭은 시스틴에게 숲에 호랑이가 있다고 이야기 합니다. 그러자 시스틴은 호랑이를 풀어주자고 제안합니다. 롭은 꿈에서 호랑이가 우리에서 나와 날아오르는 장면을 보게 되고, 호랑이를 놓아준다면 자신의 슬픔도 함께 날아갈 것이라고 믿습니다.

이 책은 슬픔으로 가득한 롭이 우리에 갇힌 호랑이에게 동정을 느끼고 그를 풀어주면서 스스로 마음을 치유하는 과정을 보여주고 있습니다. 뉴베리상 수상 작가인 케이트 디카밀로가 이 책을 통해 보내는 힐링 메시지는 독자들에게도 잔잔한 위로를 건넵니다.

원서 본문

내용이 담긴 원서 본문입니다.
원어민이 읽는 일반 원서와 같은 텍스트지만, 암기해야 할 중요 어휘들은 볼드체로 표시되어 있습니다. 이 어휘들은 지금 들고 계신 워크북에 챕터별로 정리되어 있습니다.

학습 심리학 연구 결과에 따르면, 한 단어씩 따로 외우는 단어 암기는 거의 효과가 없다고 합니다. 단어를 제대로 외우기 위해서는 문맥(context) 속에서 단어를 암기해야 하며, 한 단어당 문맥 속에서 15번 이상 마주칠 때 완벽하게 암기할 수 있다고 합니다.

이 책의 본문에서는 중요 어휘를 볼드체로 강조하여, 문맥 속의 단어들을 더 확실히 인지(word cognition in context)하도록 돕고 있습니다. 또한 대부분의 중요 단어들은 다른 챕터에서도 반복해서 등장하기 때문에 이 책을 읽는 것만으로도 자연스럽게 어휘력을 향상시킬 수 있습니다.

또한 본문 하단에는 내용 이해를 돕기 위한 '각주'가 첨가되어 있습니다. 각주는 굳이 암기할 필요는 없지만, 알아 두면 도움이 될 만한 정보를 설명하고 있습니다. 각주를 참고하면 스토리를 더 깊이 있게 이해할 수 있어 원서를 읽는 재미가 배가됩니다.

워크북(Workbook)

Check Your Reading Speed

해당 챕터의 단어 수가 기록되어 있어, 리딩 속도를 측정할 수 있습니다. 특히 리딩 속도를 중시하는 독자들이 유용하게 사용할 수 있습니다.

Build Your Vocabulary

본문에 볼드 표시되어 있는 단어들이 정리되어 있습니다. 리딩 전·후에 반복해서 보면 원서를 더욱 쉽게 읽을 수 있고, 어휘력도 빠르게 향상될 것입니다.

단어는 〈스펠링 – 빈도 – 발음기호 – 품사 – 한글 뜻 – 영문 뜻〉 순서로 표기되어 있으며 빈도 표시(★)가 많을수록 필수 어휘입니다. 반복해서 등장하는 단어는 빈도 대신 '복습'으로 표기되어 있습니다. 품사는 아래와 같이 표기했습니다

n. 명사 │ a. 형용사 │ ad. 부사 │ vi. 자동사 │ vt. 타동사 │ v. 자·타동사 모두 쓰이는 동사

conj. 접속사 │ prep. 전치사 │ int. 감탄사 │ phrasal v. 구동사 │ idiom 숙어 및 관용구

Comprehension Quiz

간단한 퀴즈를 통해 읽은 내용에 대한 이해력을 점검해 볼 수 있습니다.

「뉴베리 컬렉션」 이렇게 읽어 보세요!

아래와 같이 프리뷰(Preview) → 리딩(Reading) → 리뷰(Review) 세 단계를 거치면서 읽으면, 더욱 효과적으로 영어 실력을 향상할 수 있습니다.

1. 프리뷰(Preview) : 오늘 읽을 내용을 먼저 점검하자!

• 워크북을 통해 오늘 읽을 챕터에 나와 있는 단어들을 쭉 훑어봅니다. 어떤 단어들이 나오는지, 내가 아는 단어와 모르는 단어는 어떤 것들이 있는지 가벼운 마음으로 살펴봅니다.

• 평소처럼 하나하나 쓰면서 암기하려고 하지는 마세요! 익숙하지 않은 단어들을 주의 깊게 보되, 어차피 리딩을 하면서 점차 익숙해질 단어라는 것을 기억하며 빠르게 훑어봅니다.

• 뒤 챕터로 갈수록 '복습'이라고 표시된 단어들이 늘어나는 것을 알 수 있습니다. '복습' 단어인데도 여전히 익숙하지 않다면 더욱 신경을 써서 봐야겠죠? 매일매일 꾸준히 읽는다면, 익숙한 단어들이 점점 많아진다는 것을 몸으로 느낄 수 있습니다.

2. 리딩(Reading) : 내용에 집중하며 빠르게 읽어 나가자!

• 프리뷰를 마친 후 바로 리딩을 시작합니다. 방금 살펴봤던 어휘들을 문장 속에서 다시 만나게 되는데, 이 과정에서 단어의 쓰임새와 어감을 자연스럽게 익히게 됩니다.

• 모르는 단어나 이해되지 않는 문장이 나오더라도 멈추지 말고 전체적인 맥락을 파악하면서 속도감 있게 읽어 나가세요. 이해되지 않는 문장들은 따로 표시를 하되, 일단 넘어가고 계속 읽는 것이 좋습니다. 뒷부분을 읽다 보면 자연히 이해가 되는 경우도 있고, 정 이해가 되지 않는 부분은 리딩을 마친 이후에 따로 리뷰하는 시간을 가지면 됩니다. 문제집을 풀듯이 모든 문장을 분석하면서 원서를 읽는 것이 아니라, 리딩을 할 때는 리딩에만, 리뷰를 할 때는 리뷰에만 집중하는 것이 필요합니다.

• 볼드 처리된 단어의 의미가 궁금하더라도 워크북을 바로 펼치지 마세요. 정 궁금하다면 한 번씩 참고하는 것도 나쁘진 않지만, 워크북과 원서를 번갈아 보면서 읽는 것은 리딩의 흐름을 끊고 단어 하나하나에 집착하는 좋지 않은 리딩 습관을 심어 줄 수 있습니다.

• 같은 맥락에서 번역서를 구해 원서와 동시에 번갈아 보는 것도 좋은 방법이 아닙니다. 한글 번역을 가지고 있다고 해도 일단 영어로 읽을 때는 영어에만 집중하고 어느 정도 분량을 읽은 후에 번역서와 비교하도록 하세요.

10

모든 문장을 일일이 번역해서 완벽하게 이해하려는 것은 오히려 좋지 않은 리딩 습관을 심어 주어 장기적으로는 바람직하지 않은 결과를 얻을 수 있습니다. 처음부터 완벽하게 이해하려고 하는 것보다는 빠른 속도로 2~3회 반복해서 읽는 방식이 실력 향상에 더 도움이 됩니다. 만일 반복해서 읽어도 내용이 전혀 이해되지 않아 곤란하다면 책 선정에 문제가 있다고 할 수 있습니다. 그럴 때는 좀 더 쉬운 책을 골라 실력을 다진 뒤 다시 도전하는 것이 좋습니다.

• 초보자라면 분당 150단어의 리딩 속도를 목표로 잡고 리딩을 합니다. 분당 150단어는 원어민이 말하는 속도로, 영어 학습자들이 리스닝과 스피킹으로 넘어가기 위해 가장 기초적으로 달성해야 하는 단계입니다. 분당 50~80단어 정도의 낮은 리딩 속도를 가지고 있는 경우는 대부분 영어 실력이 부족해서라기보다 '잘못된 리딩 습관'을 가지고 있어서 그렇습니다. 이해력이 조금 떨어진다고 하더라도 분당 150단어까지는 속도에 대한 긴장감을 놓치지 말고 속도감 있게 읽어 나가도록 하세요.

3. 리뷰(Review) : 이해력을 점검하고 꼼꼼하게 다시 살펴보자!

• 해당 챕터의 Comprehension Quiz를 통해 이해력을 점검해 봅니다.

• 오늘 만난 어휘들을 다시 한번 복습합니다. 이때는 읽으면서 중요하다고 생각했던 단어를 연습장에 써 보면서 꼼꼼하게 외우는 것도 좋습니다.

• 이해가 되지 않는다고 표시해 두었던 부분도 주의 깊게 분석해 봅니다. 다시 한번 문장을 꼼꼼히 읽고, 어떤 이유에서 이해가 되지 않았는지 생각해 봅니다. 따로 메모를 남기거나 노트를 작성하는 것도 좋은 방법입니다.

• 사실 꼼꼼히 리뷰하는 것은 매우 고된 과정입니다. 원서를 읽고 리뷰하는 시간을 가지는 것이 영어 실력 향상에 많은 도움이 되기는 하지만, 이 과정을 철저히 지키려다가 원서 읽기의 재미를 반감시키는 것은 바람직하지 않습니다. 그럴 때는 차라리 리뷰를 가볍게 하는 것이 좋을 수 있습니다. '내용에 빠져서 재미있게', 문제집에서는 상상도 못할 '많은 양'을 읽으면서, 매일매일 조금씩 꾸준히 실력을 키워 가는 것이 원서를 활용하는 기본적인 방법이며, 영어 공부의 왕도입니다. 문제집 풀듯이 원서 읽기를 시도하고 접근해서는 실패할 수밖에 없습니다.

• 이런 방식으로 원서를 끝까지 다 읽었다면, 다시 반복해서 읽거나 오디오북을 활용하는 등 다양한 방식으로 원서 읽기를 확장해 나갈 수 있습니다. 이에 대한 자세한 안내가 워크북 말미에 실려 있습니다.

1. What did Rob think of the Kentucky Star sign where he waited for the bus?
   A. He thought it looked nothing like Kentucky.
   B. He thought that it would make him homesick.
   C. He liked it and thought it would bring him luck.
   D. He hated it and thought it was unlucky.

2. What was Rob doing in the woods when he found the tiger?
   A. He had been wandering and not really looking for anything.
   B. He had heard about the tiger and wanted to see for himself.
   C. He was meeting his best friend before school.
   D. He was helping his father with work before school.

3. What did Rob imagine himself as having in order to contain his emotions?
   A. A backpack
   B. A suitcase
   C. A paper bag
   D. A closet

4. How did Norton and Billy Threemonger treat Rob?

    A. They were kind and polite to him.

    B. They were mean and bullied Rob.

    C. They acted like best friends with each other.

    D. They completely ignored Rob and left him alone.

5. What did Rob think of on the bus in order not to cry?

    A. He thought about his mother.

    B. He thought about the rash on his legs.

    C. He thought about the tiger.

    D. He thought about his homework.

6. What did the bus driver do that was surprising to the boys?

    A. He stopped Norton and Billy from bullying Rob.

    B. He stopped the bus until Norton and Billy apologized to Rob.

    C. He stopped the bus at a gas station.

    D. He stopped the bus and picked up a new student.

Chapter One

Check Your Reading Speed

1분에 몇 단어를 읽는지 리딩 속도를 측정해보세요.

$$\frac{690 \text{ words}}{\text{reading time ( ) sec}} \times 60 = (\quad) \text{ WPM}$$

Build Your Vocabulary

compose**
[kəmpóuz]
vt. 구성하다, 조립하다; (마음을) 가라앉히다, 가다듬다
The things that something is composed of are its parts or members.

harbor*
[háːrbər]
v. (생각·계획 등을) 마음속에 품다; 숨기다, 숨겨주다; n. 피난처, 은신처; 항구, 항만
If you harbor an emotion, thought, or secret, you have it in your mind over a long period of time.

dim*
[dim]
a. 흐릿한, 어둑한, 희미한; v. 어둑하게 하다, 흐려지다
If you have a dim memory or understanding of something, it is difficult to remember or is unclear in your mind.

abiding
[əbáidiŋ]
a. 지속적인, 변치않는
An abiding feeling, memory, or interest is one that you have for a very long time.

notion*
[nóuʃən]
n. 생각, 개념, 관념
A notion is an idea or belief about something.

wander*
[wándər]
v. 돌아다니다, 어슬렁거리다; n. 유랑, 방랑
If you wander in a place, you walk around there in a casual way, often without intending to go in any particular direction.

board***
[bɔːrd]
v. (문·창문 등을) 판자로 막다[대다]; n. 판자, 널
If a window or a door is boarded, it is covered with boards.

tumble*
[tʌmbl]
v. 떨어지다, 넘어지다; 재주넘다; n. 넘어지기, 구르기; 재주넘기
If someone or something tumbles somewhere, they fall there with a rolling or bouncing movement.

pace*
[peis]
v. 왔다 갔다 하다, 천천히 걷다; n. 걸음걸이; 속도
If you pace a small area, you keep walking up and down it, because you are anxious or impatient.

stare*
[stɛər]
v. 응시하다, 뚫어지게 보다
If you stare at someone or something, you look at them for a long time.

trap*
[træp]
v. 가두다, 함정에 빠뜨리다; n. 덫, 함정
If you are trapped somewhere, something falls onto you or blocks your way and prevents you from moving or escaping.

still***
[stil]
a. 정지한, 움직이지 않는; 조용한, 고요한; ad. 여전히, 아직도
If air or water is still, it is not moving.

14

trick**
[trik]

n. 묘기, 마술; 비결, 요령; v. 속이다; 장난치다
A trick is an action that is intended to deceive someone.

mist**
[mist]

n. 안개; v. 안개가 끼다, 눈이 흐려지다
Mist consists of a large number of tiny drops of water in the air, which make it difficult to see very far.

astound*
[əstáund]

vt. 몹시 놀라게 하다, 망연자실하게 하다 (astounded a. 몹시 놀란)
If something astounds you, you are very surprised by it.

amaze*
[əméiz]

vt. 깜짝 놀라게 하다 (amazed a. 놀란)
If something amazes you, it surprises you very much.

doubt***
[daut]

v. 의심하다, 의혹을 품다; n. 의심; 회의
If you have doubt or doubts about something, you feel uncertain about it and do not know whether it is true or possible.

beat***
[bi:t]

v. (심장이) 고동치다; 때리다, 치다, 두드리다; 패배시키다; 이기다; n. [음악] 박자
When your heart or pulse beats, it continually makes regular rhythmic movements.

beneath**
[biní:θ]

prep. ~의 아래[밑]에, ~보다 낮은
Something that is beneath another thing is under the other thing.

rash
[ræʃ]

① n. 발진, 뾰루지 ② a. (언동이) 무분별한, 경솔한; 성급한, 조급한
A rash is an area of red spots that appears on your skin when you are ill or have a bad reaction to something that you have eaten or touched.

itch*
[itʃ]

n. 가려움; vi. 가렵다, 근질근질하다 (itchy a. 가려운, 가렵게 하는)
An itch is an uncomfortable feeling on your skin that makes you want to rub it with your nails.

blister
[blístər]

n. 물집, 수포; 부품; v. 물집이 생기다
A blister is a painful swelling on the surface of your skin. Blisters contain a clear liquid and are usually caused by heat or by something repeatedly rubbing your skin.

snake**
[sneik]

v. 꿈틀거리다, 꾸불꾸불 나아가다; n. 뱀
If you sneak somewhere, you go there very quietly on foot, trying to avoid being seen or heard.

funeral*
[fjú:nərəl]

n. 장례식
A funeral is the ceremony that is held when the body of someone who has died is buried or cremated.

heave*
[hi:v]

v. (규칙적으로 크게) 들썩거리다; (한숨을) 내쉬다; 들어올리다
If something heaves, it moves up and down with large regular movements.

sob*
[sab]

n. 흐느낌, 오열; v. 흐느껴 울다
A sob is one of the noises that you make when you are crying.

slap*
[slæp]

v. 찰싹 때리다; 탁 놓다; n. 찰싹 (때림)
If you slap someone, you hit them with the palm of your hand.

rip *
[rip]

v. 찢다, 벗겨내다; 돌진하다; n. 찢어진 틈, 잡아 찢음
When something rips or when you rip it, you tear it forcefully with your hands or with a tool such as a knife.

afterward *
[ǽftərwərd]

ad. 나중에, 그 뒤에
If you do something or if something happens afterward, you do it or it happens after a particular event or time that has already been mentioned.

specific *
[spisífik]

a. 명확한, 구체적인, 특정의 (specifically ad. 명확하게, 특히)
You use specific to refer to a particular fixed area, problem, or subject.

chain **
[tʃein]

v. 사슬로 매다; n. 쇠사슬; 연쇄, 일련
If a person or thing is chained to something, they are fastened to it with a chain.

starve **
[sta:rv]

v. 굶주리다, 굶어죽다
If people starve, they suffer greatly from lack of food which sometimes leads to their death.

guard **
[ga:rd]

n. 경계, 감시; 경호원, 호위자; v. 지키다, 망보다 (guard dog n. 경비견)
A guard is someone such as a soldier, police officer, or prison officer who protects or watches a particular place or person.

eager ***
[íːgər]

a. 열망하는, 간절히 하고 싶어 하는
If you are eager to do or have something, you want to do or have it very much.

suitcase *
[súːtkèis]

n. 여행 가방
A suitcase is a box or bag with a handle and a hard frame in which you carry your clothes when you are traveling.

stuff *
[stʌf]

vt. 채워 넣다, 속을 채우다; n. 물건, 물질
If you stuff a container or space with something, you fill it with something or with a quantity of things until it is full.

sullen *
[sʌ́lən]

a. (날씨·소리·색이) 음침한; 뚱한, 시무룩한
If the sky is sullen, it is darkened by clouds.

blink *
[bliŋk]

v. 눈을 깜박거리다; (등불·별 등이) 깜박이다; n. 깜박거림
When you blink or when you blink your eyes, you shut your eyes and very quickly open them again.

unaffected
[ʌnəféktid]

a. (~의) 영향을 받지 않은, 마음이 흔들리지 않는; 마음으로부터의, 진실한
If someone or something is unaffected by an event or occurrence, they are not changed by it in any way.

strain *
[strein]

v. 필사적이다, 안간힘을 쓰다; 잡아당기다; 팽팽하게 하다; 한계에 이르다;
n. 팽팽함, 긴장
If you strain to do something, you make a great effort to do it when it is difficult to do.

16

Chapter Two

Check Your Reading Speed

1분에 몇 단어를 읽는지 리딩 속도를 측정해보세요.

$$\frac{480 \text{ words}}{\text{reading time (\quad) sec}} \times 60 = (\quad) \text{ WPM}$$

Build Your Vocabulary

aisle[*]
[ail]

n. 통로, 측면의 복도
An aisle is a long narrow gap that people can walk along between rows of seats in a public building.

block[***]
[blak]

v. (지나가지 못하게) 막다, 차단하다; n. (단단한) 사각형 덩어리
To block a road, channel, or pipe means to put an object across it or in it so that nothing can pass through it or along it.

shrug[*]
[ʃrʌg]

v. (어깨를) 으쓱하다; n. (양 손바닥을 내보이면서 어깨를) 으쓱하기
If you shrug, you raise your shoulders to show that you are not interested in something or that you do not know or care about something.

slip[*]
[slip]

v. 미끄러지듯이 들어가다[움직이다], 미끄러지다; 재빨리 입다; 슬며시 두다
If you slip somewhere, you go there quickly and quietly.

metallic[*]
[mətǽlik]

a. 금속의, 금속성의
Metallic means consisting entirely or partly of metal.

rot[*]
[rat]

v. 썩다, 썩이다; n. 썩음, 부패 (rotten a. 썩은, 부패한)
When food, wood, or another substance rots, or when something rots it, it becomes softer and is gradually destroyed.

glow[*]
[glou]

v. 빛을 내다, 빛나다; n. 빛, 밝음
If something glows, it produces a dull, steady light.

brim[*]
[brim]

n. (모자의) 챙; 가장자리, 테두리; v. 넘치다, 넘치려고 하다
The brim of a hat is the wide part that sticks outward at the bottom.

shove[*]
[ʃʌv]

v. 밀치다, 떠밀다, 밀어내다; n. 밀치기
If you shove something somewhere, you push it there quickly and carelessly.

swagger[*]
[swǽgər]

vi. 뽐내며 걷다; 으스대다
If you swagger, you walk in a very proud, confident way, holding your body upright and swinging your hips.

lean[**]
[liːn]

① v. 몸을 구부리다, 기울다; 기대다, 의지하다 ② a. 야윈, 마른
When you lean in a particular direction, you bend your body in that direction.

grab[*]
[græb]

v. 부여잡다, 움켜쥐다; n. 부여잡기
If you grab something, you take it or pick it up suddenly and roughly.

grind* [graind]

v. (ground–ground) 비벼 문지르다, 갈다, 찧다, 빻다
If you grind something, you make it smooth or sharp by rubbing it against a hard surface.

knuckle [nʌkl]

n. 손가락 관절[마디]; v. 손가락 마디로 치다
Your knuckles are the rounded pieces of bone that form lumps on your hands where your fingers join your hands, and where your fingers bend.

scalp [skælp]

n. 두피, 머리가죽
Your scalp is the skin under the hair on your head.

bore* [bɔ:r]

v. 지루하게[따분하게] 만들다 (bored a. 지루해[따분해]하는)
If you are bored, you feel tired and impatient because you have lost interest in something or because you have nothing to do.

pretend* [priténd]

v. 가장하다, ~인 체하다; a. 가짜의
If you pretend that something is the case, you act in a way that is intended to make people believe that it is the case, although in fact it is not.

stare^{복습} [steər]

v. 응시하다, 뚫어지게 보다
If you stare at someone or something, you look at them for a long time.

whistle** [hwisl]

v. 휘파람 불다; n. 휘파람; 호각
When you whistle or when you whistle a tune, you make a series of musical notes by forcing your breath out between your lips, or your teeth.

on one's own

idiom 혼자서, 단독으로
When you are on your own, you are alone.

creep* [kri:p]

vi. 기다, 살금살금 걷다; n. 포복
If something creeps somewhere, it moves very slowly.

crud [krʌd]

n. 상처에서 피나 진물이 나와 말라붙어 생긴 딱지
Crud is any unpleasant external ailment, disorder, as a skin rash.

gross* [grous]

a. 역겨운, 구역질나는; 전체의
If you describe something as gross, you think it is very unpleasant.

concentrate** [kánsəntrèit]

v. 집중하다, 전념하다
If you concentrate on something, you give all your attention to it.

drive* [draiv]

v. (어떤 상태·행위에) 빠지게[이르게] 하다; 몰다, 몰아넣다; 운전하다
(drive someone wild idiom ~을 흥분시키다)
To drive someone into a particular state or situation means to force them into that state or situation.

lurch [lə:rtʃ]

v. 휘청하다, 요동치다, 비틀거리다
To lurch means to make a sudden movement, especially forward, in an uncontrolled way.

route** [ru:t]

n. 길, 노선; 수단, 방법; v. 보내다, 발송하다
A route is a way from one place to another.

18

punch[**]
[pʌntʃ]

v. 세게 치다, 강타하다, 두드리다; (키를) 입력하다; n. 주먹질, 펀치
If you punch someone or something, you hit them hard with your fist.

ignore[**]
[ignɔ́:r]

vt. 무시하다, 모르는 체하다
If you ignore someone or something, you pay no attention to them.

swing[**]
[swiŋ]

v. (swung–swung) 빙 돌다, 돌리다; 흔들(리)다
If something swings in a particular direction or if you swing it in that direction, it moves in that direction with a smooth, curving movement.

open-mouthed
[óupən-máuðd]

a. 몹시 놀란; 입을 벌린
If someone is looking open-mouthed, they are staring at something with their mouth wide open because it has shocked, frightened, or excited them.

lacy
[léisi]

a. 레이스로 된; 레이스 같은
Lacy things are made from lace or have pieces of lace attached to them.

1. What was the girl wearing when she got on the bus?
   A. A white school uniform
   B. A T-shirt and jeans
   C. An orange dress with pink polka dots
   D. A pink lacy dress

2. What did Sistine use as a reference for her name?
   A. The Sistine Tower
   B. The Sistine Chapel
   C. The Sistine Palace
   D. The Sistine Art Museum

3. Which of the following is NOT something that Rob thought about as he looked outside the window at school?
   A. The tiger
   B. God and Adam
   C. Sistine
   D. The rash

4. How did Sistine feel about the South and why?
    A. She loved the South, because the people were friendly.
    B. She loved the South, because the weather was warm.
    C. She hated the South, because the people were ignorant.
    D. She hated the South, because the weather was warm.

5. What did Rob's mom teach him to do when she was sick?
    A. She taught him how to paint portraits.
    B. She taught him how to whistle songs.
    C. She taught him how to whittle wood.
    D. She taught him how to cook dinner.

6. What was Rob doing in class when he was called to the principal's office?
    A. He was drawing a picture of the tiger.
    B. He was working on his homework for the next class.
    C. He was writing a story about the tiger.
    D. He was playing a video game about tigers.

7. How did Sistine act toward Rob as he left class?
    A. She looked worried for him.
    B. She shot him a look of pure hate.
    C. She shot him a smile full of warmth.
    D. She waved goodbye in a friendly way.

Chapter Three

Check Your Reading Speed

1분에 몇 단어를 읽는지 리딩 속도를 측정해보세요.

$$\frac{474 \text{ words}}{\text{reading time ( ) sec}} \times 60 = (\quad) \text{ WPM}$$

Build Your Vocabulary

lacy^{복습}
[léisi]

a. 레이스로 된; 레이스 같은
Lacy things are made from lace or have pieces of lace attached to them.

aisle^{복습}
[ail]

n. 통로, 측면의 복도
An aisle is a long narrow gap that people can walk along between rows of seats in a public building.

gravelly
[grǽvəli]

a. (목소리가) 불쾌한, 귀에 거슬리는; 자갈이 많은
A gravelly voice is low and rather rough and harsh.

clipped
[klipt]

a. (말하는 태도가) 딱 부러지는
If you say that someone has a clipped way of speaking, you mean they speak with quick, short sounds, and usually that they sound upper-class.

stamp^{**}
[stamp]

v. (기계로 어떤 모양을) 찍다, (도장 등을) 찍다; 쿵쿵거리며 걷다, 발을 구르다;
n. 우표; 도장, 스탬프
If you stamp a mark or word on an object, you press the mark or word onto the object using a stamp or other device.

elbow^{**}
[élbou]

vt. 팔꿈치로 쿡 찌르다; n. 팔꿈치
If you elbow people aside or elbow your way somewhere, you push people with your elbows in order to move somewhere.

rib[*]
[rib]

n. 늑골, 갈빗대; [요리] 갈비
Your ribs are the 12 pairs of curved bones that surround your chest.

thud
[θʌd]

n. 쿵, 털썩(무거운 물건이 떨어지는 소리); v. (둔탁한 소리를 내며) 쿵 떨어지다
A thud is a dull sound, such as that a heavy object makes when it hits something soft.

sway[*]
[swei]

v. 흔들(리)다, 동요하다; 설득하다; n. 동요
When people or things sway, they lean or swing slowly from one side to the other.

stare^{복습}
[stɛər]

v. 응시하다, 뚫어지게 보다
If you stare at someone or something, you look at them for a long time.

fault^{**}
[fɔːlt]

n. 잘못, 책임; 결점, 흠; v. 나무라다, 흠을 잡다
If a bad or undesirable situation is your fault, you caused it or are responsible for it.

chin[**]
[tʃín]

n. 아래턱, 턱 끝
Your chin is the part of your face that is below your mouth and above your neck.

hoot
[huːt]

v. 야유하다, 콧방귀 끼다; 경적을 울리다; (올빼미 등이) 울다;
n. 외침소리, 폭소; 올빼미 울음소리
If you hoot, you make a loud high-pitched noise when you are laughing or showing disapproval.

chapel[*]
[tʃǽpəl]

n. 채플, 예배; 예배당
A chapel is a building used for worship by members of some Christian churches. Chapel refers to the religious services that take place there.

amaze[복습]
[əméiz]

vt. 깜짝 놀라게 하다 (amazed a. 놀란)
If something amazes you, it surprises you very much.

cuff
[kʌf]

① v. (손바닥으로 살짝) 치다, 때리다
② v. ~에 수갑을 채우다; n. 수갑; (상의나 셔츠의) 소매 끝동
If you cuff someone, you strike or beat them with your open hand.

disease[**]
[dizíːz]

n. 병, 질환
A disease is an illness which affects people, animals, or plants, for example one which is caused by bacteria or infection.

swagger[복습]
[swǽgər]

vi. 뽐내며 걷다; 으스대다
If you swagger, you walk in a very proud, confident way, holding your body upright and swinging your hips.

whisper[*]
[hwíspəːr]

v. 속삭이다; n. 속삭임; 속삭이는 소리
When you whisper, you say something very quietly.

slick
[slik]

a. 매끈매끈한, 반들반들한; 멋진, 호화로운; 능숙한, 교묘한
Something is slick means it is smooth and glossy.

reward[**]
[riwɔ́ːrd]

n. 보상, 보답; 현상금, 보상금; v. 보답하다, 보상하다
A reward is something that you are given, for example because you have behaved well, worked hard, or provided a service to the community.

ceiling[**]
[síːliŋ]

n. 천장
A ceiling is the horizontal surface that forms the top part or roof inside a room.

highway[*]
[háiwèi]

n. 고속도로
A highway is a main road, especially one that connects towns or cities.

rash[복습]
[ræʃ]

① n. 발진, 뾰루지 ② a. (언동이) 무분별한, 경솔한; 성급한, 조급한
A rash is an area of red spots that appears on your skin when you are ill or have a bad reaction to something that you have eaten or touched.

suitcase[복습]
[súːtkèis]

n. 여행 가방
A suitcase is a box or bag with a handle and a hard frame in which you carry your clothes when you are traveling.

Chapter Four

Check Your Reading Speed

1분에 몇 단어를 읽는지 리딩 속도를 측정해보세요.

$$\frac{485 \text{ words}}{\text{reading time ( ) sec}} \times 60 = (\qquad) \text{ WPM}$$

Build Your Vocabulary

gravelly^{복습}
[grǽvəli]

a. (목소리가) 불쾌한, 귀에 거슬리는; 자갈이 많은
A gravelly voice is low and rather rough and harsh.

planet[*]
[plǽnit]

n. 행성
A planet is a large, round object in space that moves around a star.

snort[*]
[snɔːrt]

v. (경멸 등으로) 콧방귀 뀌다, 콧김을 뿜다; n. 거센 콧김
People sometimes snort in order to express disapproval or amusement.

giggle[*]
[gigl]

v. 낄낄 웃다; n. 낄낄 웃음
If someone giggles, they laugh in a childlike way, because they are amused, nervous, or embarrassed.

ignorant^{**}
[ignərənt]

a. 무지한, 무식한; 무례한
If you describe someone as ignorant, you mean that they do not know things they should know.

defiant
[difáiənt]

a. 도전적인, 반항적인, 시비조의 (defiantly ad. 도전적으로)
If you say that someone is defiant, you mean they show aggression or independence by refusing to obey someone.

put one's foot in one's mouth

idiom 큰 실수를 하다, 실언을 하다
If someone puts their feet in it or puts their feet in their mouths, they accidentally do or say something which embarrasses or offends people.

farther^{**}
[fáːrðər]

ad. (far–farther–farthest) 더 나아가서, 더 멀리
Farther means to a greater extent or degree.

glare[*]
[glɛər]

v. 노려보다; 번쩍번쩍 빛나다; n. 노려봄; 섬광
If you glare at someone, you look at them with an angry expression on your face.

stick^{**}
[stik]

① v. (stuck–stuck) 내밀다; 찔러 넣다, 찌르다; 달라붙다, 붙이다; 고수하다
② n. 막대기, 지팡이
If something is sticking out from a surface or object, it extends up or away from it.

whittle
[hwitl]

vt. (나무를) 조금씩 깎다, 깎아서 어떤 모양을 만들다
If you whittle something from a piece of wood, you carve it by cutting pieces off the wood with a knife.

edge**
[edʒ]

n. 끝, 가장자리, 모서리
The edge of something is the place or line where it stops, or the part of it that is furthest from the middle.

jiggle
[dʒigl]

v. 좌우[상하]로 급히 움직이(게 하)다; 가볍게 흔들다, 가볍게 당기다
If you jiggle something, you move it quickly up and down or from side to side.

principal*
[prínsəpəl]

n. 장(長), 교장; a. 주요한, 제1의
The principal of a school is the person in charge of the school.

trip***
[trip]

v. 걸려 넘어지(게 하)다; 경쾌한 걸음걸이로 걷다; n. 여행
If you trip someone who is walking or running, you put your foot or something else in front of them, so that they knock their own foot against it and fall or nearly fall.

Chapters Five & Six

1. How did Mr. Phelmer begin his talks with Rob?
   A. He was always worried.
   B. He was always glad.
   C. He was always surprised.
   D. He was always angry.

2. Why were some of the parents concerned about Rob?
   A. They thought that Rob's father did not care about him.
   B. They thought that Rob needed more friends at school.
   C. They thought that Rob was a bully and should be nicer.
   D. They thought that Rob's rash might be contagious.

3. What did Mr. Phelmer tell Rob would be a good idea?
   A. He could go to the school nurse between classes.
   B. He could stay home until his rash went away.
   C. He could go to the hospital for surgery on his legs.
   D. He could wear long pants from then on.

4. How did Rob feel about it when he left the principal's office?

    A. He felt shocked.

    B. He felt tired.

    C. He felt free.

    D. He felt bored.

5. What did Rob do when the crowd of children surrounded Sistine?

    A. He ignored it and worked on his tiger drawing.

    B. He told them to leave Sistine alone.

    C. He told Sistine to run.

    D. He went to go find a teacher to stop a fight from happening.

6. What did Rob do when the children confronted him directly?

    A. He ran away from them.

    B. He fought back.

    C. He screamed and cried.

    D. He slowly walked away.

7. Which of the following items did Rob keep in his pocket that truly mattered to him?

    A. A letter from Sistine

    B. A note from Mr. Phelmer

    C. The drawing of the tiger

    D. A knife for whittling

Chapter Five

Check Your Reading Speed

1분에 몇 단어를 읽는지 리딩 속도를 측정해보세요.

$$\frac{617\ words}{reading\ time\ (\quad)\ sec} \times 60 = (\quad)\ WPM$$

Build Your Vocabulary

principal^{복습}
[prínsəpəl]

n. 장(長), 교장; a. 주요한, 제1의
The principal of a school is the person in charge of the school.

secretary[*]
[sékrətèri]

n. 비서, 서기; 사무관, 비서관
A secretary is a person who is employed to do office work, such as typing letters, answering phone calls, and arranging meetings.

nod^{**}
[nɔd]

v. 끄덕이다, 끄덕여 표시하다; n. (동의·인사·신호·명령의) 끄덕임
If you nod, you move your head downward and upward to show agreement, understanding, or approval.

wave^{**}
[weiv]

v. 흔들다, 신호하다; 파도치다; n. 흔들기, 흔드는 신호; 파도, 물결
If you wave or wave your hand, you move your hand from side to side in the air, usually in order to say hello or goodbye to someone.

throat^{**}
[θrout]

n. 목(구멍) (clear one's throat idiom 목을 가다듬다)
Your throat is the back of your mouth and the top part of the tubes that go down into your stomach and your lungs.

pat[*]
[pæt]

v. (애정을 담아) 쓰다듬다; 톡톡 가볍게 치다; n. 쓰다듬기
If you pat something or someone, you tap them lightly, usually with your hand held flat.

comb[*]
[koum]

v. (머리카락·동물의 털 등을) 빗질하다, 빗다; (장소 등을) 철저히 수색하다; n. 빗
When you comb your hair, you tidy it using a comb.

bald[*]
[bɔːld]

a. (머리 등이) 벗어진, 대머리의; vi. 머리가 벗어지다
Someone who is bald has little or no hair on the top of their head.

interact
[intərǽkt]

vi. 교류하다, 상호 작용하다
When people interact with each other, they communicate as they spend time together.

panel[*]
[pǽnl]

vt. (벽·방 등에) 판자를 대다; (배심원을) 선정하다; n. 틀, 판자
(paneled a. 장식 판자를 댄)
A paneled wall, door, or window does not have a flat surface but has square or rectangular areas set into its surface.

astonish[*]
[əstániʃ]

vt. 깜짝 놀라게 하다 (astonishing a. 놀라운, 눈부신)
If something or someone astonishes you, they surprise you very much.

array[*]
[əréi]

n. 모음, 무리; 배열, 정렬; vt. 정렬시키다, 배열하다
An array of different things or people is a large number or wide range of them.

frame**
[freim]

vt. 테에 끼우다, ~의 뼈대를 만들다, 짜 맞추다; n. 구조, 골격, 틀
When a picture or photograph is framed, it is put in a frame.

certificate*
[sərtífikət]

n. 증명서
A certificate is an official document stating that particular facts are true.

diploma*
[diplóumə]

n. 졸업 증서
A diploma is a document showing that you have completed a course of study or part of your education.

crack**
[kræk]

v. 날카로운 소리가 나게 하다; 금이 가다, 깨다; n. 날카로운 소리; 갈라진 금
If something cracks, or if you crack it, it makes a sharp sound like the sound of a piece of wood breaking.

knuckle복습
[nʌkl]

n. 손가락 관절[마디]; v. 손가락 마디로 치다
Your knuckles are the rounded pieces of bone that form lumps on your hands where your fingers join your hands, and where your fingers bend.

contagious
[kəntéidʒəs]

a. 전염성의; 잘 번지는
A contagious disease spreads by people touching each other.

stuff복습
[stʌf]

n. 물건, 물질; vt. 채워 넣다, 속을 채우다
You can use stuff to refer to things such as a substance, a collection of things, events, or ideas, or the contents of something in a general way without mentioning the thing itself by name.

up-front
[ʌp-frʌnt]

a. 솔직한, 정직한; 선행 투자의, 선불의
If you are up-front about something, you act openly or publicly so that people know what you are doing or what you believe.

kick in

phrasal v. (약이) 효과가 있다, 효과를 발휘하다
If something kicks in, it starts to work or have an effect.

concentrate복습
[kánsəntrèit]

v. 집중하다, 전념하다
If you concentrate on something, you give all your attention to it.

scratch*
[skrætʃ]

v. 긁다; 할퀴다, 생채기를 내다; n. 긁기; 긁힌 자국, 긁는 소리
If you scratch yourself, you rub your fingernails against your skin because it is itching.

adjust**
[ədʒʌst]

v. (옷매무새 등을) 바로 하다; 적응하다; 조절하다, 조정하다
If you adjust something such as your clothing or a machine, you correct or alter its position or setting.

Check Your Reading Speed

1분에 몇 단어를 읽는지 리딩 속도를 측정해보세요.

$$\frac{695 \text{ words}}{\text{reading time ( ) sec}} \times 60 = (\quad) \text{ WPM}$$

Build Your Vocabulary

float**
[flout]

v. 떠다니다; 뜨다; 띄우다; n. 뜨는 물건, 부유물
Something that floats in or through the air hangs in it or moves slowly and gently through it.

buoy
[bu:i]

v. 기운을 북돋우다; 띄우다, 띄워 두다; n. 부이, 부표
If someone in a difficult situation is buoyed by something, it makes them feel more cheerful and optimistic.

unfold*
[ʌnfóuld]

v. 펴다, 펼치다; 열리다
If someone unfolds something which has been folded or if it unfolds, it is opened out and becomes flat.

itch**습
[itʃ]

vi. 근질근질하다, 가렵다; n. 가려움
If you are itching to do something, you are very eager or impatient to do it.

swing**습
[swiŋ]

v. 흔들(리)다; 빙 돌다, 돌리다
If something swings or if you swing it, it moves repeatedly backward and forward or from side to side from a fixed point.

high-pitched
[hai-pítʃt]

a. 음조가 높은
A high-pitched sound is shrill and high in pitch.

buzz*
[bʌz]

n. 윙윙거리는 소리; v. 윙윙거리다; 분주하게 돌아다니다
You can use buzz to refer to a long continuous sound, usually caused by lots of people talking at once.

cricket*
[kríkit]

n. [곤충] 귀뚜라미
A cricket is a brown or black insect which makes short loud noises by rubbing its wings together.

fade**
[feid]

vi. 희미해지다, 바래다, 시들다 (faded a. 색이 바랜)
When a colored object fades or when the light fades it, it gradually becomes paler.

march***
[ma:rtʃ]

① v. 당당하게 걷다, 행진하다; n. 행진, 행군 ② n. 3월
If you say that someone marches somewhere, you mean that they walk there quickly and in a determined way, for example because they are angry.

yell*
[jel]

v. 소리치다, 고함치다; n. 고함소리, 부르짖음
If you yell, you shout loudly, usually because you are excited, angry, or in pain.

fist[*]
[fist]

n. (쥔) 주먹
Your hand is referred to as your fist when you have bent your fingers in toward the palm in order to hit someone.

twirl
[twəːrl]

v. 빠르게 돌다, 빙빙 돌리다; n. 회전
If you twirl, you turn around and around quickly, for example when you are dancing.

crumple
[krʌmpl]

v. 구기다, 쭈글쭈글하게 하다; 구겨지다; n. 주름
If you crumple something such as paper or cloth, or if it crumples, it is squashed and becomes full of untidy creases and folds.

wad
[wad]

v. 뭉치다; n. 뭉치, 다발
If you wad something such as paper or cloth up, you fold or press it into a tight mass.

mutter[*]
[mʌtər]

v. 중얼거리다, 불평하다; n. 중얼거림, 불평
If you mutter, you speak very quietly so that you cannot easily be heard, often because you are complaining about something.

gravelly^{복습}
[grǽvəli]

a. (목소리가) 불쾌한, 귀에 거슬리는; 자갈이 많은
A gravelly voice is low and rather rough and harsh.

stick^{복습}
[stik]

① v. (stuck–stuck) 달라붙다, 붙이다; 내밀다; 찔러 넣다, 찌르다; 고수하다
② n. 막대기, 지팡이
If you stick one thing to another, you attach it using glue, sticky tape, or another sticky substance.

forehead[*]
[fɔ́ːrhèd]

n. 이마
Your forehead is the area at the front of your head between your eyebrows and your hair.

sweat^{**}
[swet]

n. 땀; v. 땀 흘리다; 습기가 차다
Sweat is the salty colorless liquid which comes through your skin when you are hot, ill, or afraid.

shove^{복습}
[ʃʌv]

v. 밀치다, 떠밀다, 밀어내다; n. 밀치기
If you shove something somewhere, you push it there quickly and carelessly.

chase^{**}
[ʧeis]

v. 뒤쫓다, 추적하다; 추구하다; n. 추적; 추구
If you chase someone, or chase after them, you run after them or follow them quickly in order to catch or reach them.

pump^{**}
[pʌmp]

v. 상하로 (왕복하며) 움직이다, 재빠르게 움직이다; 퍼 올리다, 솟구치다
If you pumps something, you move it up and down.

thrill[*]
[θril]

n. 전율, 오싹함; v. 감동[흥분]시키다; 오싹하(게 하)다
If something gives you a thrill, it gives you a sudden feeling of great excitement, pleasure, or fear.

gym^{**}
[dʒim]

n. (= gymnasium) 체육관; (= gymnastics) 체조, 체육
A gym is a club, building, or large room, usually containing special equipment, where people go to do physical exercise and get fit.

matter^{***}
[mǽtər]

vi. 중요하다; n. 물질, 문제, 일
If you say that something does matter, you mean that it is important to you because it does have an effect on you or on a particular situation.

1. Why did Sistine sit next to Rob on the bus?
    A. She wanted to thank Rob for helping her.
    B. She wanted to protect Rob from Norton and Billy.
    C. It was the last empty seat on the bus.
    D. It was near the air conditioner.

2. How did Sistine react to the rash on Rob's legs and hearing that it was contagious?
    A. She acted disgusted and immediately changed seats.
    B. She worried that she might catch it from sitting near him.
    C. She was worried and promised to find a cure for him.
    D. She wanted to catch it and put her hand on Rob's legs.

3. What did Sistine offer to do for Rob?
    A. She offered to bring his homework to him.
    B. She offered to bring him medicine for the rash on his legs.
    C. She offered to help him fight bullies at school.
    D. She offered to help him become a professional artist.

4. How did Rob's father react to the letter from the principal?
   A. He was worried that Rob's rash might really be contagious.
   B. He was upset because he had already told him it wasn't contagious.
   C. He was annoyed that the principal thought he was a bad father.
   D. He was shocked that the principal cared about Rob so much.

5. Why did Rob's father NOT let Rob go out in the rain?
   A. He didn't want the rain to wash away the medicine on Rob's legs.
   B. He didn't want the rain to ruin Rob's clothes.
   C. He knew about the tiger and wanted Rob to stay away from it.
   D. He wanted Rob to stay in and help him cook dinner.

6. What did Rob carve from the wood while having a clear image of the tiger in his mind?
   A. He carved a tiger.
   B. He carved a bird.
   C. He carved Sistine.
   D. He carved his mother.

7. How did the tiger appear in Rob's dream?
   A. He was free and running through the woods with Sistine on his back.
   B. He was free and running through the woods with Rob on his back.
   C. He was in a cage and staring at Rob and Sistine.
   D. He was in a cage quietly sleeping.

Check Your Reading Speed

1분에 몇 단어를 읽는지 리딩 속도를 측정해보세요.

$$\frac{724 \text{ words}}{\text{reading time (\quad) sec}} \times 60 = (\quad) \text{ WPM}$$

Build Your Vocabulary

turn out

phrasal v. 결국은 ~이 되다, 결국은 ~임이 밝혀지다
That something turns out means it happens in a particular way or has a particular result.

extraordinary*
[ikstrɔ́:rdənèri]

a. 기이한, 놀라운; 비상한, 비범한
If you describe something as extraordinary, you mean that it is very unusual or surprising.

tear**
[tɛər]

① v. (tore–torn) 찢다, 찢어지다; 부리나케 가다; n. 찢음 ② n. 눈물
If you tear paper, cloth, or another material, or if it tears, you pull it into two pieces or you pull it so that a hole appears in it.

muddy**
[mʌ́di]

v. ~을 진흙투성이로 만들다; a. 진흙의; 흐린, 탁한; 흐리멍덩한
If you muddy something, you cause it to be covered in mud.

scrape*
[skreip]

n. 긁힌 자국; 문지르기, 스치기; v. 긁다, 스쳐서 상처를 내다, 문지르다
A scrape is a scratched area where the skin is torn or worn off.

stare복습
[stɛər]

v. 응시하다, 뚫어지게 보다
If you stare at someone or something, you look at them for a long time.

shrug복습
[ʃrʌg]

v. (어깨를) 으쓱하다; n. (양 손바닥을 내보이면서 어깨를) 으쓱하기
If you shrug, you raise your shoulders to show that you are not interested in something or that you do not know or care about something.

demand***
[dimǽnd]

vt. 묻다, 요구하다, 청구하다; n. 요구, 수요
If you demand something such as information or action, you ask for it in a very forceful way.

hick
[hik]

a. 촌스러운, 시골뜨기의
You can use hick to refer to something awkwardly simple and provincial.

immediately**
[imí:diətli]

ad. 곧바로, 즉시
If something happens immediately, it happens without any delay.

regret**
[rigrét]

vt. 후회하다, 유감으로 생각하다; n. 후회, 유감
If you regret something that you have done, you wish that you had not done it.

policy*
[pálǝsi]

n. 방침, 방책; 정책
A policy is a set of ideas or plans that is used as a basis for making decisions, especially in politics, economics, or business.

34

maintain[**]
[meintéin]

vt. 지속하다, 유지하다; 주장하다
If you maintain something, you continue to have it, and do not let it stop or grow weaker.

bet[*]
[bet]

v. ~라고 확신하다; 걸다, 내기를 하다; n. 내기, 건 돈
You use expressions such as 'I bet', 'I'll bet', and 'you can bet' to indicate that you are sure something is true.

sneer[*]
[sniər]

v. 비웃다, 냉소하다; n. 비웃음, 냉소
If you sneer at someone or something, you express your contempt for them by the expression on your face or by what you say.

narrow[***]
[nǽrou]

v. 작게 하다, 좁히다; a. 폭이 좁은; 편협한
If your eyes narrow or if you narrow your eyes, you almost close them, for example because you are angry or because you are trying to concentrate on something.

ceiling[복습]
[síːliŋ]

n. 천장
A ceiling is the horizontal surface that forms the top part or roof inside a room.

spell[**]
[spel]

① n. 주문, 마법 ② v. (낱말을) 맞춤법에 따라 쓰다, 철자를 말하다
A spell is a situation in which events are controlled by a magical power.

on account of

idiom ~때문에, ~이므로
You use on account of to introduce the reason or explanation for something.

contagious[복습]
[kəntéidʒəs]

a. 전염성의; 잘 번지는
A contagious disease spreads by people touching each other.

astound[복습]
[əstáund]

vt. 몹시 놀라게 하다, 망연자실하게 하다 (astounding a. 놀라게 하는)
If something astounds you, you are very surprised by it.

whisper[복습]
[hwíspəːr]

v. 속삭이다; n. 속삭임; 속삭이는 소리
When you whisper, you say something very quietly.

ignore[복습]
[ignɔ́ːr]

vt. 무시하다, 모르는 체하다
If you ignore someone or something, you pay no attention to them.

disease[복습]
[dizíːz]

n. 병, 질환
A disease is an illness which affects people, animals, or plants, for example one which is caused by bacteria or infection.

apart[**]
[əpáːrt]

ad. (~와) 떨어져, 따로따로
When people or things are apart, they are some distance from each other.

sweat[복습]
[swet]

n. 땀; v. 땀 흘리다; 습기가 차다
Sweat is the salty colorless liquid which comes through your skin when you are hot, ill, or afraid.

exhaust[**]
[igzɔ́ːst]

n. (자동차 등의) 배기가스; vt. 기진맥진하게 만들다; 다 써 버리다, 고갈시키다
Exhaust is the gas or steam that is produced when the engine of a vehicle is running.

rub**
[rʌb]

v. 비비다, 문지르다; 스치다; n. 문지르기
If you rub a part of your body, you move your hand or fingers backward and forward over it while pressing firmly.

permanent**
[pə́:rmənənt]

a. 영구적인, 변하지 않는
Something that is permanent lasts forever.

on one's feet

idiom (경제적으로) 독립하여; 일어서서, 서 있는 상태로
If someone has to stand on their feet, they have to be independent and manage their lives without help from other people.

spot**
[spat]

vt. 발견하다, 분별하다; n. 반점, 얼룩; 장소, 지점
If you spot something or someone, you notice them.

relieve*
[rilíːv]

vt. (걱정·고통 등을) 덜다, 안도하게 하다, 완화하다
(relieved a. 안도하는, 다행으로 여기는)
If something relieves an unpleasant feeling or situation, it makes it less unpleasant or causes it to disappear completely.

thump
[θʌmp]

n. (세게) 치기; 쿵[탁] 하는 소리; v. 치다, 두드리다
A thump is a hitting action with loud and dull sounds.

end up

phrasal v. (구어) 마침내는 (~으로) 되다, 끝나다
If you end up doing something or end up in a particular state, you do that thing or get into that state even though you did not originally intend to.

beat*복습
[biːt]

v. 때리다, 치다, 두드리다; (심장이) 고동치다; 패배시키다, 이기다; n. [음악] 박자
If you beat someone or something, you hit them very hard.

Check Your Reading Speed

1분에 몇 단어를 읽는지 리딩 속도를 측정해보세요.

$$\frac{825 \text{ words}}{\text{reading time (} \quad \text{) sec}} \times 60 = (\quad) \text{ WPM}$$

Build Your Vocabulary

still 복습
[stil]
a. 정지한, 움직이지 않는; 조용한, 고요한; ad. 여전히, 아직도
If you stay still, you stay in the same position and do not move.

rub 복습
[rʌb]
v. 비비다, 문지르다; 스치다; n. 문지르기
If you rub a part of your body, you move your hand or fingers backward and forward over it while pressing firmly.

sigh *
[sai]
v. 한숨 쉬다; n. 한숨, 탄식
When you sigh, you let out a deep breath, as a way of expressing feelings such as disappointment, tiredness, or pleasure.

rhythm **
[riðm]
n. 리듬
A rhythm is a regular series of sounds or movements.

stuff 복습
[stʌf]
n. 물건, 물질; vt. 채워 넣다; 속을 채우다
You can use stuff to refer to things such as a substance, a collection of things, events, or ideas, or the contents of something in a general way without mentioning the thing itself by name.

principal 복습
[prínsəpəl]
n. 장(長), 교장; a. 주요한, 제1의
The principal of a school is the person in charge of the school.

nod 복습
[nɔd]
v. 끄덕이다, 끄덕여 표시하다; n. (동의·인사·신호·명령의) 끄덕임
If you nod, you move your head downward and upward to show agreement, understanding, or approval.

appointment **
[əpɔ́intmənt]
n. 예약, 약속; 지정, 임명
If you have an appointment with someone, you have arranged to see them at a particular time, usually in connection with their work or for a serious purpose.

twirl 복습
[twə:rl]
v. 빠르게 돌다, 빙빙 돌리다; n. 회전
If you twirl, you turn around and around quickly, for example when you are dancing.

punch 복습
[pʌntʃ]
v. 세게 치다, 강타하다, 두드리다; (키를) 입력하다; n. 주먹질, 펀치
If you punch someone or something, you hit them hard with your fist.

vision **
[víʒən]
n. 환상; 상상력; 시력, 통찰력
If you have a vision of someone in a particular situation, you imagine them in that situation, for example because you are worried that it might happen, or hope that it will happen.

in the meantime

idiom 그 동안에
In the meantime or meantime means in the period of time between two events.

maintenance*
[méintənəns]

n. 관리, 유지, 점검 (maintenance-man n. 보수공, 수리원)
The maintenance of a building, vehicle, road, or machine is the process of keeping it in good condition by regularly checking it and repairing it when necessary.

sweep**
[swi:p]

v. 청소하다; 쓸어내리다; 휩쓸어 가다; 휙 지나가다; (감정 등이) 엄습하다;
n. 한 번 휘두름; 청소
If you sweep an area of floor or ground, you push dirt or rubbish off it using a brush with a long handle.

ragged*
[rǽgid]

a. 몹시 지친; (옷 등이) 찢어진; 남루한, 초라한; (호흡 등이) 거친, 고르지 못한
If you are ragged, it means you are worn out from stress or strain.

slather
[slǽðə:r]

v. 듬뿍 바르다, 두껍게 칠하다
If you slather something with a substance, or slather a substance onto something, you put the substance on in a thick layer.

slap*복습
[slæp]

v. 탁 놓다; 찰싹 때리다; n. 찰싹 (때림)
If you slap something onto a surface, you put it there quickly, roughly, or carelessly.

fishy
[fíʃi]

a. 생선 냄새가 나는, 비린내 나는; 수상한
A fishy taste or smell reminds you of fish.

ointment
[ɔintmənt]

n. 연고, 고약(膏藥)
An ointment is a smooth thick substance that is put on sore skin or a wound to help it heal.

pretend*복습
[priténd]

v. 가장하다, ~인 체하다; a. 가짜의
If you pretend that something is the case, you act in a way that is intended to make people believe that it is the case, although in fact it is not.

pace*복습
[peis]

v. 왔다 갔다 하다, 천천히 걷다; n. 걸음걸이; 속도
If you pace a small area, you keep walking up and down it, because you are anxious or impatient.

desperate**
[déspərit]

a. 필사적인; 자포자기의; 절망적인 (desperately ad. 필사적으로)
If you are desperate for something or desperate to do something, you want or need it very much indeed.

mist*복습
[mist]

n. 안개; v. 안개가 끼다; 눈이 흐려지다
Mist consists of a large number of tiny drops of water in the air, which make it difficult to see very far.

rain***
[rein]

v. 비 오듯 쏟아지다; 비가 오다; n. 비
If someone rains blows, kicks, or bombs on a person or place, the person or place is attacked by many blows, kicks, or bombs.

relieve*복습
[rilí:v]

vt. (걱정·고통 등을) 덜다, 안도하게 하다, 완화하다
(relieved a. 안도하는, 다행으로 여기는)
If something relieves an unpleasant feeling or situation, it makes it less unpleasant or causes it to disappear completely.

supper[***]
[sʌ́pər]

n. 저녁 식사, (가벼운) 만찬
Supper is a simple meal eaten just before you go to bed at night.

stick[복습]
[stik]

① v. (stuck-stuck) 달라붙다, 붙이다; 내밀다; 찔러 넣다, 찌르다; 고수하다
② n. 막대기, 지팡이
If you stick one thing to another, you attach it using glue, sticky tape, or another sticky substance.

powdery
[páudəri]

a. 가루 같은, 가루의
Something that is powdery looks or feels like powder.

stove[*]
[stouv]

n. (요리용) 레인지; 난로, 스토브
A stove is a piece of equipment which provides heat, either for cooking or for heating a room.

recliner
[rikláinər]

n. (= recliner chair) 안락의자, 기대는 것
A recliner is a type of armchair having a back that can be adjusted to slope at various angles.

snore[*]
[snɔ:r]

v. 코를 골다
When someone who is asleep snores, they make a loud noise each time they breathe.

crooked
[krúkid]

a. 구부러진, 비뚤어진; 마음이 비뚤어진, 부정직한
If you describe something as crooked, especially something that is usually straight, you mean that it is bent or twisted.

jerk[*]
[dʒə:rk]

① v. 갑자기 움직이다; n. 갑자기 움직임; 반사 운동 ② n. 바보, 멍청이
If you jerk something or someone in a particular direction, or they jerk in a particular direction, they move a short distance very suddenly and quickly.

tremble[*]
[trembl]

v. (공포·추위·피로 등으로) 떨(리)다; 흔들리다; n. 떨림; 진동
If something trembles, it shakes slightly.

growl[*]
[graul]

v. 으르렁거리다; n. 으르렁거리는 소리
If someone growls something, they say something in a low, rough, and angry voice.

carve[*]
[ka:rv]

vt. 새기다, 조각하다
If you carve an object, you make it by cutting it out of a substance such as wood or stone.

skinny
[skíni]

a. 바싹 여윈, 깡마른
A skinny person is extremely thin, often in a way that you find unattractive.

stay up

phrasal v. 자지 않고 일어나 있다; 그대로 있다
If you stay up, you remain out of bed at a time when most people have gone to bed or at a time when you are normally in bed yourself.

wave[복습]
[weiv]

v. 흔들다, 신호하다; 파도치다; n. 흔들기, 흔드는 신호; 파도, 물결
If you wave or wave your hand, you move your hand from side to side in the air, usually in order to say hello or goodbye to someone.

Chapters Nine & Ten

1. Why did Rob's father wake him up so early?
   A. Rob had to catch the bus to school.
   B. Rob had to help father's work.
   C. Rob had a doctor's appointment for his rash.
   D. Rob had to go to town to find a job.

2. What else did Rob keep in his suitcase along with not-thoughts?
   A. He also had not-wishes.
   B. He also had not-fears.
   C. He also had not-memories.
   D. He also had not-goals.

3. Why did the rain NOT bother Rob?
   A. Rob thought the rain was good for his skin.
   B. Rob tried to avoid getting sunburns.
   C. Rainy days reminded him of his mother.
   D. Sunny days reminded him of his mother's funeral day.

4. What did Willie May say she would rather clean up after and why?
   A. She said she would rather clean up after dogs, because dogs at least were cute.
   B. She said she would rather clean up after dogs, because dogs at least were friendly.
   C. She said she would rather clean up after pigs, because pigs at least give respect.
   D. She said she would rather clean up after pigs, because pigs at least are quiet.

5. Why did Willie May tell Rob about school?
   A. She told him to leave school so he could start making money soon.
   B. She told him to stay in school so he could get a better job than working at a motel.
   C. She told him to only go to the classes that he liked.
   D. She told him that he should go to a private academy instead.

6. How did Willie May say that Rob could cure the rash on his legs?
   A. He could find a special plant in the woods and make medicine from it.
   B. He could go to a hospital in the city and see a doctor.
   C. He could let the sadness rise from his legs to his heart.
   D. He could stay in the sunlight and let it warm his skin.

7. What did Rob feel he had to do after Willie May left the room?
   A. He needed to scratch the rash on his legs.
   B. He needed to find his father for advice.
   C. He needed to finish his homework for the next day of school.
   D. He needed to tell someone about the tiger.

Check Your Reading Speed

1분에 몇 단어를 읽는지 리딩 속도를 측정해보세요.

$$\frac{704 \text{ words}}{\text{reading time ( ) sec}} \times 60 = (\quad) \text{ WPM}$$

Build Your Vocabulary

squeak*
[skwi:k]

v. 끽[찍] 하는 소리를 내다; n. 끽[찍] 하는 소리
If something or someone squeaks, they make a short, high-pitched sound.

personal***
[pɔ́rsənl]

a. 개인의, 사사로운; 자신이 직접 하는
A personal opinion, quality, or thing belongs or relates to one particular person rather than to other people.

shooting star
[ʃú:tiŋ stá:r]

n. 유성, 별똥별
A shooting star is a piece of rock or metal that burns very brightly when it enters the earth's atmosphere from space, and is seen from earth as a bright star traveling very fast across the sky.

suitcase복습
[sú:tkèis]

n. 여행 가방
A suitcase is a box or bag with a handle and a hard frame in which you carry your clothes when you are traveling.

lid*
[lid]

n. 뚜껑
A lid is the top of a box or other container which can be removed or raised when you want to open the container.

lean복습
[li:n]

① v. 기대다, 의지하다; 몸을 구부리다, 기울다 ② a. 야윈, 마른
If you lean on or against someone or something, you rest against them so that they partly support your weight.

elbow복습
[élbou]

n. 팔꿈치; vt. 팔꿈치로 쿡 찌르다
Your elbow is the part of your arm where the upper and lower halves of the arm are joined.

drum***
[drʌm]

v. 둥둥[쿵쿵] 소리를 내다[치다]; 북을 치다; n. 북, 드럼
If something drums on a surface, or if you drum something on a surface, it hits it regularly, making a continuous beating sound.

glow복습
[glou]

v. 빛을 내다, 빛나다; n. 빛, 밝음
If something glows, it produces a dull, steady light.

rub복습
[rʌb]

v. 비비다, 문지르다; 스치다; n. 문지르기
If you rub a part of your body, you move your hand or fingers backward and forward over it while pressing firmly.

swamp*
[swamp]

n. 늪, 습지; v. 궁지에 빠뜨리다; 가라앉다
A swamp is an area of very wet land with wild plants growing in it.

42

bother*
[báðər]

v. 귀찮게 하다, 괴롭히다, 폐 끼치다; 일부러 ~하다, 애를 쓰다
If something bothers you, or if you bother about it, it worries, annoys, or upsets you.

mutter^{복습}
[mʌtər]

v. 중얼거리다, 불평하다; n. 중얼거림, 불평
If you mutter, you speak very quietly so that you cannot easily be heard, often because you are complaining about something.

funeral^{복습}
[fjú:nərəl]

n. 장례식
A funeral is the ceremony that is held when the body of someone who has died is buried or cremated.

jerk^{복습}
[dʒəːrk]

① v. 갑자기 움직이다; n. 갑자기 움직임; 반사 운동 (jerky a. 홱 움직이는)
② n. 바보, 멍청이
Jerky movements are very sudden and quick, and do not flow smoothly.

desperate^{복습}
[déspərit]

a. 필사적인; 자포자기의, 절망적인
If you are desperate for something or desperate to do something, you want or need it very much indeed.

smash*
[smæʃ]

v. 세게 충돌시키다; 때려 부수다, 깨뜨리다; n. 강타; 부서지는 소리; 분쇄
If something smashes or is smashed against something solid, it moves very fast and with great force against it.

pillow*
[pílou]

n. 베개; 머리 받침대 (pillowy a. 베개 같은, 푹신한)
A pillow is a rectangular cushion which you rest your head on when you are in bed.

rock*
[rak]

① v. 앞뒤[좌우]로 흔들(리)다, 진동하다; 동요하다 ② n. 바위, 암석
When something rocks or when you rock it, it moves slowly and regularly backward and forward or from side to side.

cobweb
[kábwèb]

n. 거미집[줄]; 거미집[줄] 모양의 것 (cobwebby a. 거미집 모양의, 거미줄을 친)
A cobweb is the net which a spider makes for catching insects.

pat^{복습}
[pæt]

v. (애정을 담아) 쓰다듬다, 톡톡 가볍게 치다; n. 쓰다듬기
If you pat something or someone, you tap them lightly, usually with your hand held flat.

extend^{**}
[iksténd]

v. (손·발 등을) 뻗다, 늘이다; 넓히다, 확장하다; 주다, 베풀다
If someone extends their hand, they stretch out their arm and hand to shake hands with someone.

rip^{복습}
[rip]

v. 찢다, 벗겨내다; 돌진하다; n. 찢어진 틈, 잡아 찢음
When something rips or when you rip it, you tear it forcefully with your hands or with a tool such as a knife.

split^{**}
[split]

v. 찢다, 째다, 쪼개다; n. 쪼개기, 분열; 금, 균열
If something splits or if you split it, it is divided into two or more parts.

slap^{복습}
[slæp]

v. 찰싹 때리다; 탁 놓다; n. 찰싹 (때림)
If you slap someone, you hit them with the palm of your hand.

remind^{**}
[rimáind]

vt. 생각나게 하다, 상기시키다, 일깨우다
If someone reminds you of a fact or event that you already know about, they say something which makes you think about it.

steam** [stiːm]
n. 증기; v. 증기가 발생하다; (식품 등을) 찌다
Steam is the hot mist that forms when water boils.

curl** [kəːrl]
vt. 소용돌이치며 올라가다; 꼬다, 곱슬곱슬하게 하다; n. 컬, 곱슬머리
If something curls somewhere, or if you curl it there, it moves there in a spiral or curve.

sip* [sip]
vt. (음료를) 홀짝거리다, 조금씩 마시다; n. 한 모금
If you sip a drink or sip at it, you drink by taking just a small amount at a time.

bitter** [bítər]
a. 맛이 쓴; 격렬한; 쓰라린
A bitter taste is sharp, not sweet, and often slightly unpleasant.

maintenance^{복습} [méintənəns]
n. 관리, 유지, 점검
The maintenance of a building, vehicle, road, or machine is the process of keeping it in good condition by regularly checking it and repairing it when necessary.

shed* [ʃed]
① n. 오두막, 헛간 ② v. 없애다, 버리다
A shed is a small building that is used for storing things such as garden tools.

whistle^{복습} [hwisl]
v. 휘파람 불다; n. 휘파람; 호각
When you whistle or when you whistle a tune, you make a series of musical notes by forcing your breath out between your lips, or your teeth.

mine** [main]
v. 채굴하다; n. 광산; 지뢰
When a mineral such as coal, diamonds, or gold is mined, it is obtained from the ground by digging deep holes and tunnels.

swoop* [swuːp]
v. 급강하하다, 내리 덮치다; n. 급강하
When a bird or airplane swoops, it suddenly moves downward through the air in a smooth curving movement.

solid** [sálid]
a. 단단한; 견실한, 견고한; n. 고체
A solid substance or object stays the same shape whether it is in a container or not.

curse** [kəːrs]
vt. 욕설을 퍼붓다, 저주하다; n. 저주, 악담
If you curse, you use rude or offensive language, usually because you are angry about something.

flick [flik]
n. 가볍게 치기; vt. 가볍게 치다, 튀기다; 잽싸게 움직이다
If you flick something such as a whip or a towel, or flick something with it, you hold one end of it and move your hand quickly up and then forward, so that the other end moves.

catch up
phrasal v. 따라잡다, 따라가다
If you catch up with someone, you reach them by walking faster than them.

44

Check Your Reading Speed

1분에 몇 단어를 읽는지 리딩 속도를 측정해보세요.

$$\frac{692 \text{ words}}{\text{reading time (\quad) sec}} \times 60 = (\quad) \text{ WPM}$$

Build Your Vocabulary

sweep^{복습}
[swi:p]

v. 청소하다; 쓸어내리다; 휩쓸어 가다; 휙 지나가다; (감정 등이) 엄습하다;
n. 청소; 한 번 휘두름
If you sweep an area of floor or ground, you push dirt or rubbish off it using a brush with a long handle.

laundry*
[lɔ́:ndri]

n. 세탁물; 세탁소 (laundry room n. 세탁실)
Laundry is used to refer to clothes, sheets, and towels that are about to be washed, are being washed, or have just been washed.

housekeeper*
[hauskí:pər]

n. 가정부; 주부
A housekeeper is a person whose job is to cook, clean, and look after a house for its owner.

adjust^{복습}
[ədʒʌ́st]

v. (옷매무새 등을) 바로 하다; 적응하다; 조절하다, 조정하다
If you adjust something such as your clothing or a machine, you correct or alter its position or setting.

barn**
[ba:rn]

n. 헛간, 축사
A barn is a building on a farm in which crops or animal food can be kept.

respect**
[rispékt]

n. 존경, 경의; 주의, 관심; v. 존경하다, 소중히 여기다
If you have respect for someone, you have a good opinion of them.

broom*
[bru:m]

n. 빗자루, 비
A broom is a kind of brush with a long handle. You use a broom for sweeping the floor.

smooth**
[smu:ð]

a. 매끄러운, 반들반들한; 유창한; v. 매끄럽게 하다[되다]
A smooth surface has no roughness, lumps, or holes.

carve^{복습}
[ka:rv]

vt. 새기다, 조각하다
If you carve an object, you make it by cutting it out of a substance such as wood or stone.

cheekbone
[tʃí:kbòun]

n. 광대뼈
Your cheekbones are the two bones in your face just below your eyes.

slant*
[slænt]

v. 기울(게 하)다, 경사지(게 하)다; a. 기울어진, 비스듬한; n. 경사, 비탈
(slanted a. 기울어진, 치우친)
Something that slants is sloping, rather than horizontal or vertical.

narrow 복습
[nǽrou]

v. 작게 하다, 좁히다; a. 폭이 좁은; 편협한
If your eyes narrow or if you narrow your eyes, you almost close them, for example because you are angry or because you are trying to concentrate on something.

shrug 복습
[ʃrʌg]

v. (어깨를) 으쓱하다; n. (양 손바닥을 내보이면서 어깨를) 으쓱하기
If you shrug, you raise your shoulders to show that you are not interested in something or that you do not know or care about something.

skinny 복습
[skíni]

a. 바싹 여윈, 깡마른
A skinny person is extremely thin, often in a way that you find unattractive.

end up 복습

phrasal v. (구어) 마침내는 (~으로) 되다, 끝나다
If you end up doing something or end up in a particular state, you do that thing or get into that state even though you did not originally intend to.

**cigarette*
[sigərét]

n. 담배
Cigarettes are small tubes of paper containing tobacco which people smoke.

light*
[lait]

v. (lit/lighted—lit/lighted) 불을 붙이다, 불이 붙다; 빛을 비추다; n. 빛
If you light something such as a cigarette or fire, or if it lights, it starts burning.

**scent*
[sent]

n. 냄새, 향기; v. 냄새로 찾아내다, 냄새 맡다; 향기가 나다
The scent of something is the pleasant smell that it has.

on account of 복습

idiom ~때문에, ~이므로
You use on account of to introduce the reason or explanation for something.

cure*
[kjuər]

vt. 치료하다, 고치다; n. 치료, 치료법
If doctors or medical treatments cure a person, they make the person well again after an illness or injury.

chew*
[ʧu:]

v. 씹다, 씹어서 으깨다
If you chew gum, you keep biting it and moving it around your mouth to taste the flavor of it.

heal*
[hi:l]

v. (상처·아픔·고장 등을) 낫게 하다, 치료하다
When something heals it, it becomes healthy and normal again.

relieve 복습
[rilí:v]

vt. (걱정·고통 등을) 덜다, 안도하게 하다, 완화하다
(relieved a. 안도하는, 다행으로 여기는)
If something relieves an unpleasant feeling or situation, it makes it less unpleasant or causes it to disappear completely.

principal 복습
[prínsəpəl]

n. 장(長), 교장; a. 주요한, 제1의
The principal of a school is the person in charge of the school.

contagious 복습
[kəntéidʒəs]

a. 전염성의; 잘 번지는
A contagious disease spreads by people touching each other.

certificate복습
[sərtífikət]

n. 증명서
A certificate is an official document stating that particular facts are true.

offer***
[ɔ́ːfər]

v. (의견·이유 등을) 말하다, 제의[제안]하다; 제공하다; n. 제공
If you offer someone information, advice, or praise, you give it to them.

frame복습
[freim]

vt. 테에 끼우다, ~의 뼈대를 만들다, 짜 맞추다; n. 구조, 골격, 틀
When a picture or photograph is framed, it is put in a frame.

bet복습
[bet]

v. ~라고 확신하다; 걸다, 내기를 하다; n. 내기, 건 돈
You use expressions such as 'I bet', 'I'll bet', and 'you can bet' to indicate that you are sure something is true.

stretch**
[stretʃ]

v. 쭉 펴다, 뻗다, 늘이다; n. (특히 길게 뻗은) 길, 구간; 뻗침
When you stretch, you put your arms or legs out straight and tighten your muscles.

tower*
[tauər]

vi. 높이 솟다; n. 탑
Someone or something that towers over surrounding people or things is a lot taller than they are.

poem**
[pouəm]

n. 시, 운문
A poem is a piece of writing in which the words are chosen for their beauty and sound and are carefully arranged, often in short lines which rhyme.

rhythm복습
[ríðm]

n. 리듬
A rhythm is a regular series of sounds or movements.

swirl*
[swəːrl]

n. 소용돌이, 빙글빙글 돌기; vi. 소용돌이치다, 빙빙 돌다
A swirl of something is a shape of something rotating rapidly.

doubt복습
[daut]

v. 의심하다, 의혹을 품다; n. 의심; 회의
If you have doubt or doubts about something, you feel uncertain about it and do not know whether it is true or possible.

capable**
[kéipəbl]

a. (능력·특질상) ~을 할 수 있는; 유능한
If a person or thing is capable of doing something, they have the ability to do it.

1. Why was the motel called Kentucky Star?
    A. It was named after a famous signer.
    B. It was the name of the owner's old racehorse.
    C. It was a place where many people from Kentucky stayed.
    D. It was the name of a comic book hero.

2. When Rob told Sistine about the tiger, how did she react?
    A. She asked if it were real.
    B. She asked if he were crazy.
    C. She simply laughed at him.
    D. She simply asked where.

3. How did Rob feel about telling Sistine about the tiger?
    A. He thought that he should have told Willie May about it too.
    B. He wished he had told his father first.
    C. He knew he had picked the right person.
    D. He thought that he should have just kept it his secret.

4. Why did Sistine and Rob have to visit the motel before seeing the tiger?
   A. Rob wanted to bring his father's gun for protection.
   B. Rob wanted to bring a notebook to draw a picture of the tiger.
   C. Sistine needed to call her mother and tell her where she was going.
   D. Sistine needed to change out of her dress into Rob's clothes.

5. How did Sistine react to Rob's wood carving of her?
   A. She thought it was creepy.
   B. She thought it was perfect.
   C. She thought it looked nothing like her.
   D. She thought that she could carve better than Rob.

6. Which of the following is one of the not-wishes buried deepest inside of Rob?
   A. The wish for a friend
   B. The wish for a girlfriend
   C. The wish for a pet tiger
   D. The wish for a sister

Check Your Reading Speed

1분에 몇 단어를 읽는지 리딩 속도를 측정해보세요.

$$\frac{513 \text{ words}}{\text{reading time ( ) sec}} \times 60 = (\quad) \text{ WPM}$$

Build Your Vocabulary

weed˚
[wi:d]

v. 잡초를 뽑다; n. 잡초
If you weed an area, you remove the weeds from it.

crackᵇᵏ
[kræk]

n. 갈라진 금; 날카로운 소리; v. 금이 가다, 깨다; 날카로운 소리가 나게 하다
A crack is a very narrow gap between two things, or between two parts of a thing.

sidewalk˚
[sáidwɔ:k]

n. (포장한) 보도, 인도
A sidewalk is a path with a hard surface by the side of a road.

rumble
[rʌmbl]

v. (차 등이) 덜거덕거리며 가다; 우르르 울리(게 하)다; n. 우르르 하는 소리; 소음
If a vehicle rumbles somewhere, it moves slowly forward while making a low continuous noise.

yellᵇᵏ
[jel]

v. 소리치다, 고함치다; n. 고함소리, 부르짖음
If you yell, you shout loudly, usually because you are excited, angry, or in pain.

concentrateᵇᵏ
[kánsəntrèit]

v. 집중하다, 전념하다
If you concentrate on something, you give all your attention to it.

diseaseᵇᵏ
[dizí:z]

n. 병, 질환
A disease is an illness which affects people, animals, or plants, for example one which is caused by bacteria or infection.

rotᵇᵏ
[rat]

v. 썩다, 썩이다; n. 썩음, 부패
When food, wood, or another substance rots, or when something rots it, it becomes softer and is gradually destroyed.

stareᵇᵏ
[stɛər]

v. 응시하다, 뚫어지게 보다
If you stare at someone or something, you look at them for a long time.

spit˚
[spit]

v. 뱉다, 내뿜다
If you spit liquid or food somewhere, you force a small amount of it out of your mouth.

cough˚˚
[kɔ:f]

v. (엔진이) 덜덜거리다; 기침하다; n. 기침
When you cough, you force air out of your throat with a sudden, harsh noise.

sputter
[spʌ́tə:r]

v. (엔진 등이) 털털거리는 소리를 내다; 흥분하여 말하다, 식식거리며 말하다
If something such as an engine or a flame sputters, it works or burns in an uneven way and makes a series of soft popping sounds.

roar[*]
[rɔːr]

vi. (기계 등이) 큰 소리 내며 움직이다; (큰 짐승 등이) 으르렁거리다, 고함치다;
n. 외치는 소리, 왁자지껄함; 으르렁거리는 소리
If something, usually a vehicle, roars somewhere, it goes there very fast, making a loud noise.

tear[복습]
[tɛər]

① v. (tore-torn) 찢다, 찢어지다; 부리나케 가다; n. 찢음 ② n. 눈물
If you tear paper, cloth, or another material, or if it tears, you pull it into two pieces or you pull it so that a hole appears in it.

stuff[복습]
[stʌf]

vt. 채워 넣다, 속을 채우다; n. 물건, 물질
If you stuff a container or space with something, you fill it with something or with a quantity of things until it is full.

knuckle[복습]
[nʌkl]

n. 손가락 관절[마디]; v. 손가락 마디로 치다
Your knuckles are the rounded pieces of bone that form lumps on your hands where your fingers join your hands, and where your fingers bend.

bleed[*]
[bliːd]

v. 피가 나다, 출혈하다
When you bleed, you lose blood from your body as a result of injury or illness.

determined[*]
[ditэ́ːrmind]

a. 결연한, 굳게 결심한
If you are determined to do something, you have made a firm decision to do it and will not let anything stop you.

story[**]
[stɔ́ːri]

① n. (건물의) 층 ② n. 이야기
A story of a building is one of its different levels, which is situated above or below other levels.

squat[*]
[skwat]

a. 땅딸막한; 쪼그리고 앉은; v. 웅크리다, 쪼그리고 앉다
If you describe someone or something as squat, you mean they are short and thick, usually in an unattractive way.

compose[복습]
[kəmpóuz]

vt. 구성하다, 조립하다; (마음을) 가라앉히다, 가다듬다
The things that something is composed of are its parts or members.

entire[*]
[intáiər]

a. 전체의; 완전한 (entirely ad. 완전히, 전부)
You use entire when you want to emphasize that you are referring to the whole of something, for example, the whole of a place, time, or population.

sigh[복습]
[sai]

v. 한숨 쉬다; n. 한숨, 탄식
When you sigh, you let out a deep breath, as a way of expressing feelings such as disappointment, tiredness, or pleasure.

blink[복습]
[bliŋk]

v. (등불·별 등이) 깜박이다; 눈을 깜박거리다; n. 깜박거림
When a light blinks, it flashes on and off.

equation[*]
[ikwéiʒən]

n. 등식, 방정식
An equation is a mathematical statement saying that two amounts or values are the same.

stick[복습]
[stik]

① v. 달라붙다, 붙이다; 내밀다; 찔러 넣다, 찌르다; 고수하다 ② n. 막대기, 지팡이
If you stick one thing to another, you attach it using glue, sticky tape, or another sticky substance.

scalp 복습
[skælp]

n. 두피, 머리가죽
Your scalp is the skin under the hair on your head.

droopy
[drúːpi]

a. 축 늘어진, 수그린; 지친, 의기소침한
If you describe something as droopy, you mean that it hangs down with no strength or firmness.

pinched
[pintʃt]

a. (가난 등으로) 수척해진; (돈에) 궁한, 쪼들리는
If someone's face is pinched, it looks thin and pale, usually because they are ill or old.

recognize**
[rékəgnaiz]

vt. 인지하다, 알아보다
If you recognize someone or something, you know who that person is or what that thing is.

drizzly
[drízli]

a. (비가) 보슬보슬 내리는
When the weather is drizzly, the sky is dull and gray and it rains steadily but not very hard.

fierce*
[fiərs]

a. 사나운; 격렬한, 지독한
Fierce conditions are very intense, great, or strong.

Check Your Reading Speed

1분에 몇 단어를 읽는지 리딩 속도를 측정해보세요.

$$\frac{530 \text{ words}}{\text{reading time (\quad) sec}} \times 60 = (\quad) \text{ WPM}$$

Build Your Vocabulary

doubt^{복습}
[daut]

v. 의심하다, 의혹을 품다; n. 의심; 회의 (doubtfully ad. 미심쩍게, 의심스럽게)
If you have doubt or doubts about something, you feel uncertain about it and do not know whether it is true or possible.

unmade
[ʌnméid]

a. (침대가) 정돈되어 있지 않은
An unmade bed has not had the sheets and covers neatly arranged after it was last slept in.

tatter
[tǽtəːr]

v. 해지다; 갈가리 찢다; n. 넝마, 누더기 옷 (tattered a. 해진!)
If something such as clothing or a book is tattered, it is damaged or torn, especially because it has been used a lot over a long period of time.

recliner^{복습}
[rikláinər]

n. (= recliner chair) 안락의자, 기대는 것
A recliner is a type of armchair having a back that can be adjusted to slope at various angles.

odd**
[ad]

a. 이상한, 기묘한
If you describe someone or something as odd, you think that they are strange or unusual.

bend**
[bend]

v. (bent−bent) 구부리다, 굽히다; 구부러지다, 휘다; n. 커브, 굽음
When you bend a part of your body such as your arm or leg, or when it bends, you change its position so that it is no longer straight.

particularly**
[pərtíkjələrli]

ad. 특히, 각별히
You use particularly to indicate that what you are saying applies especially to one thing or situation.

life-size
[láif-sáiz]

a. 실물 크기의
A life-size representation of someone or something, for example a painting or sculpture, is the same size as the person or thing that they represent.

accurate**
[ǽkjurət]

a. 정확한, 정밀한
Accurate information, measurements, and statistics are correct to a very detailed level.

sculpt
[skʌlpt]

v. (= sculpture) 새기다, 조각하다; n. 조각; 조각상
When an artist sculpts something, they carve or shape it out of a material such as stone or clay.

sculptor
[skʌlptəːr]

n. 조각가, 조각사
A sculptor is someone who creates sculptures.

wave ^{복습}
[weiv]

n. 파도, 물결; 흔들기, 흔드는 신호; v. 흔들다, 신호하다; 파도치다
If you refer to a wave of a particular feeling, you mean that it increases quickly and becomes very intense, and then often decreases again.

embarrass**
[imbǽrəs]

v. 부끄럽게[무안하게] 하다, 어리둥절하게 하다; 당황하다
(embarrassment n. 당황, 난처)
If something or someone embarrasses you, they make you feel shy or ashamed.

light ^{복습}
[lait]

v. (lit/lighted–lit/lighted) 불을 붙이다, 불이 붙다; 빛을 비추다; n. 빛
If you light something such as a cigarette or fire, or if it lights, it starts burning.

rash ^{복습}
[ræʃ]

① n. 발진, 뾰루지 ② a. (언동이) 무분별한, 경솔한; 성급한, 조급한
A rash is an area of red spots that appears on your skin when you are ill or have a bad reaction to something that you have eaten or touched.

rub ^{복습}
[rʌb]

v. 비비다, 문지르다; 스치다; n. 문지르기
If you rub a part of your body, you move your hand or fingers backward and forward over it while pressing firmly.

straighten**
[streitn]

v. 똑바르게 하다, 곧게 하다
If you straighten something, you make it tidy or put it in its proper position.

lie***
[lai]

vi. 놓여 있다, 위치하다; 눕다, 누워 있다
If an object lies in a particular place, it is in a flat position in that place.

intend***
[inténd]

v. ~할 작정이다, ~하려고 생각하다; 의도하다
If you intend to do something, you have decided or planned to do it.

defiant ^{복습}
[difáiənt]

a. 도전적인, 반항적인, 시비조의
If you say that someone is defiant, you mean they show aggression or independence by refusing to obey someone.

stance
[stæns]

n. 발의 자세, 스탠스
Your stance is the way that you are standing.

bury**
[béri]

vt. 묻다, 파묻다, 매장하다
If something buries itself somewhere, or if you bury it there, it is pushed very deeply in there.

course**
[kɔːrs]

v. (액체가) 빠르게 흐르다; n. 진행, 진로; 과정
If something courses, it proceeds or moves quickly.

arc*
[aːrk]

n. 호, 원호
An arc is a smoothly curving line or movement.

sigh ^{복습}
[sai]

v. 한숨 쉬다; n. 한숨, 탄식
When you sigh, you let out a deep breath, as a way of expressing feelings such as disappointment, tiredness, or pleasure.

stick^{복습}
[stik]

① v. (stuck–stuck) 내밀다; 찔러 넣다, 찌르다; 달라붙다, 붙이다; 고수하다
② n. 막대기, 지팡이

If something is sticking out from a surface or object, it extends up or away from it.

relief^{***}
[rilíːf]

n. 안심, 안도

If you feel a sense of relief, you feel happy because something unpleasant has not happened or is no longer happening.

1. Why had Sistine come to Lister, Florida?
   A. Sistine had come to Lister to visit her aunt for a month.
   B. Sistine was starting a new art school in Lister to bring culture to the area.
   C. She had grown bored of living in Philadelphia, Pennsylvania.
   D. Her mother had grown up in Lister and brought Sistine after they left her father.

2. What did Rob hesitate to tell Sistine that made her upset?
   A. He hesitated to tell her about his mother.
   B. He hesitated to tell her about his father.
   C. He hesitated to tell her about his love for tigers.
   D. He hesitated to tell her about his love for her.

3. Which of the following is NOT something that came to Rob's mind as Sistine walked away from him in the woods?
   A. It was like looking into a fun-house mirror, because she was wearing his clothes.
   B. It was like watching himself walk away, because she was wearing his clothes.
   C. It reminded him of his dream of Sistine riding on the back of the tiger.
   D. It reminded him that there were wild panthers around and that the woods were dangerous.

4. Which of the following best describes the tiger's cage?
   A. It was made of thick iron bars and a steel roof with a combination lock.
   B. It was made out of wood with glass holes and a metal door with padlocks.
   C. It was made out of rusted chainlink fence with a wood board for a roof and padlocks.
   D. It was made of bamboo with three padlocks.

5. What does Sistine say is just like the tiger?
   A. A candle burning bright
   B. A poem about tigers burning bright
   C. Tigers in cages at zoos
   D. A bright orange racecar

6. Rob had come to recognize and be wary of which of Sistine's gestures?
   A. Putting her hands on her hips
   B. Staring at him without smiling
   C. Brushing the hair out of her eyes
   D. Crossing her arms over her chest

7. What feeling filled Rob as he and Sistine ran through the woods?
   A. Excitement
   B. Happiness
   C. Confusion
   D. Humor

Check Your Reading Speed

1분에 몇 단어를 읽는지 리딩 속도를 측정해보세요.

$$\frac{671 \text{ words}}{\text{reading time (} \quad \text{) sec}} \times 60 = (\quad) \text{ WPM}$$

Build Your Vocabulary

scrub
[skrʌb]

① n. 관목숲 ② n. 북북 문질러 씻기[닦기]; v. 북북 문지르다, 비벼서 씻다
Scrub consists of low trees and bushes, especially in an area that has very little rain.

cluster*
[klʌstər]

n. 무리, 떼, 집단; v. 밀집하다
A cluster of people or things is a small group of them close together.

drip*
[drip]

v. 방울방울[뚝뚝] 떨어지다; 가득[넘칠 듯이] 지니고 있다
When something drips, drops of liquid fall from it.

swing 복습
[swiŋ]

v. 흔들(리)다; 빙 돌다, 돌리다
If something swings or if you swing it, it moves repeatedly backward and forward or from side to side from a fixed point.

make it

idiom (자기 분야에서) 성공하다; ~에 도착하다
If you make it, you are successful in achieving something difficult, or in surviving through a very difficult period.

affair***
[əféər]

n. 사건; 일거리, 사무 (have an affair with idiom ~와 바람을 피우다)
If two people who are not married to each other have an affair, they have a sexual relationship.

secretary 복습
[sékrətèri]

n. 비서, 서기; 사무관, 비서관
A secretary is a person who is employed to do office work, such as typing letters, answering phone calls, and arranging meetings.

type**
[taip]

v. (편지·서류 등을) 타자하다, 타자를 치다; 분류하다; n. 활자; 유형, 타입
If you type something, you use a typewriter or word processor to write it.

drape
[dreip]

vt. (손·발 등을) 되는 대로 걸치다; 주름을 잡아 예쁘게 덮다; n. 드리워진 모양
If you drape a piece of cloth somewhere, you place it there so that it hangs down in a casual and graceful way.

suitcase 복습
[súːtkèis]

n. 여행 가방
A suitcase is a box or bag with a handle and a hard frame in which you carry your clothes when you are traveling.

will***
[wil]

v. 바라다, 원하다; 의지를 발동하다; 뜻하다; n. 의지; 유언장
If you will something to happen, you try to make it happen by using mental effort rather than physical effort.

mess up

phrasal v. 망쳐놓다, 어질러놓다
If you mess something up or if you mess up, you cause something to fail or be spoiled.

shrug^{복습}
[ʃrʌg]

v. (어깨를) 으쓱하다; n. (양 손바닥을 내보이면서 어깨를) 으쓱하기
If you shrug, you raise your shoulders to show that you are not interested in something or that you do not know or care about something.

sculpture[*]
[skʌ́lptʃər]

n. 조각, 조각상; v. 조각하다
A sculpture is an object made out of stone, wood, or clay by an artist.

protest^{**}
[prətést]

v. 항의하다, 이의를 제기하다; n. 항의
If you protest against something or about something, you say or show publicly that you object to it.

whittle^{복습}
[hwitl]

vt. (나무를) 조금씩 깎다, 깎아서 어떤 모양을 만들다 (whittling n. 깎기)
If you whittle something from a piece of wood, you carve it by cutting pieces off the wood with a knife.

argue^{***}
[áːrgjuː]

v. 주장하다, 논쟁하다
If one person argues with another, they speak angrily to each other about something that they disagree about.

jail[*]
[dʒeil]

n. 교도소, 감옥, 구치소
A jail is a place where criminals are kept in order to punish them, or where people waiting to be tried are kept.

trespass[*]
[tréspəs]

vi. 침입하다, 침해하다
If someone trespasses, they go onto someone else's land without their permission.

demand^{복습}
[dimǽnd]

vt. 묻다, 요구하다, 청구하다; n. 요구, 수요
If you demand something such as information or action, you ask for it in a very forceful way.

narrow^{복습}
[nǽrou]

v. 작게 하다, 좁히다; a. 폭이 좁은; 편협한
If your eyes narrow or if you narrow your eyes, you almost close them, for example because you are angry or because you are trying to concentrate on something.

march^{복습}
[maːrtʃ]

① v. 당당하게 걷다, 행진하다; n. 행진, 행군 ② n. 3월
If you say that someone marches somewhere, you mean that they walk there quickly and in a determined way, for example because they are angry.

bend^{복습}
[bend]

v. (bent–bent) 구부리다, 굽히다; 구부러지다, 휘다; n. 커브, 굽음
When you bend a part of your body such as your arm or leg, or when it bends, you change its position so that it is no longer straight.

scratch^{복습}
[skrætʃ]

v. 긁다, 할퀴다, 생채기를 내다; n. 긁기; 긁힌 자국, 긁는 소리
If you scratch yourself, you rub your fingernails against your skin because it is itching.

remind^{복습}
[rimáind]

vt. 생각나게 하다, 상기시키다, 일깨우다
If someone reminds you of a fact or event that you already know about, they say something which makes you think about it.

bear^{***}
[bɛər]

① v. 참다, 견디다; 낳다; (의무·책임을) 지다 ② n. 곰
If you can't bear someone or something, you dislike them very much.

ragged 복습
[rǽgid]

a. (호흡 등이) 거친, 고르지 못한; 몹시 지친; (옷 등이) 찢어진; 남루한, 초라한
You can say that something is ragged when it is untidy or uneven.

gasp *
[gǽsp]

n. 헐떡거림; v. (놀람 따위로) 숨이 막히다, 헐떡거리다
A gasp is a short quick breath of air that you take in through your mouth, especially when you are surprised, shocked, or in pain.

professional **
[prəféʃənl]

a. 전문가의 솜씨를 보이는, 능숙한; 전문적인
Professional means relating to a person's work, especially work that requires special training.

nod 복습
[nɔd]

v. 끄덕이다, 끄덕여 표시하다; n. (동의·인사·신호·명령의) 끄덕임
If you nod, you move your head downward and upward to show agreement, understanding, or approval.

Check Your Reading Speed

1분에 몇 단어를 읽는지 리딩 속도를 측정해보세요.

$$\frac{641 \text{ words}}{\text{reading time ( ) sec}} \times 60 = (\qquad) \text{ WPM}$$

Build Your Vocabulary

rust*
[rʌst]

v. (금속 등이) 녹슬다, 부식하다; n. 녹
If metal rusts or something rusts it, it becomes covered with rust.

board복습
[bɔ:rd]

n. 판자, 널; v. (문·창문 등을) 판자로 막다[대다]
A board is a flat, thin, rectangular piece of wood or plastic which is used for a particular purpose.

serve***
[sə:rv]

v. (특정한 용도로) 쓰일 수 있다; 식사 시중을 들다; (음식을) 제공하다; 근무하다; 보복하다, 인과응보다
If something serves as a particular thing or serves a particular purpose, it performs a particular function, which is often not its intended function.

padlock
[pǽdlàk]

n. 맹꽁이 자물쇠; vt. 맹꽁이 자물쇠를 채우다
A padlock is a lock which is used for fastening two things together.

pace복습
[peis]

v. 왔다 갔다 하다, 천천히 걷다; n. 걸음걸이; 속도
If you pace a small area, you keep walking up and down it, because you are anxious or impatient.

carve복습
[ka:rv]

vt. 새기다, 조각하다 (carving n. 조각물, 조각)
If you carve an object, you make it by cutting it out of a substance such as wood or stone.

order***
[ɔ́:rdər]

vt. 명령을 내리다; 주문하다; n. 주문; 명령; 순서
If a person in authority orders someone to do something, they tell them to do it.

ignore복습
[ignɔ́:r]

vt. 무시하다, 모르는 체하다
If you ignore someone or something, you pay no attention to them.

concentrate복습
[kánsəntrèit]

v. 집중하다, 전념하다
If you concentrate on something, you give all your attention to it.

enormous*
[inɔ́:rməs]

a. 엄청난, 거대한, 막대한
You can use enormous to emphasize the great degree or extent of something.

poem복습
[pouəm]

n. 시, 운문
A poem is a piece of writing in which the words are chosen for their beauty and sound and are carefully arranged, often in short lines which rhyme.

fierce복습
[fiərs]

a. 격렬한, 지독한; 사나운
Fierce conditions are very intense, great, or strong.

whirl[*]
[hwə:rl]

v. 빙글 돌다, 선회하다
If something or someone whirls around or if you whirl them around, they move around or turn around very quickly.

face[***]
[feis]

v. ~을 마주보다, 향하다; 직면하다, 직시하다
If someone or something faces a particular thing, person, or direction, they are positioned opposite them or are looking in that direction.

selfish[*]
[sélfiʃ]

a. 이기적인, 제멋대로의
If you say that someone is selfish, you mean that he or she cares only about himself or herself, and not about other people.

set free

phrasal v. (사람·동물을) 자유롭게 하다, 석방하다
If you set free someone or something, it means you grant freedom to them.

gesture[**]
[dʒéstʃər]

n. 몸짓; vi. 몸짓[제스처, 신호]을 하다
A gesture is a movement that you make with a part of your body, especially your hands, to express emotion or information.

recognize[복습]
[rékəgnaiz]

vt. 인지하다, 알아보다
If you recognize someone or something, you know who that person is or what that thing is.

wary
[wéəri]

a. 조심성 있는, 신중한
If you are wary of something or someone, you are cautious because you do not know much about them and you believe they may be dangerous or cause problems.

saw[*]
[sɔ:]

① vt. 톱으로 자르다; n. 톱 ② v. SEE의 과거·과거분사형
If you saw something, you cut it with a saw.

mere[**]
[miər]

a. (무엇이 있다는 그 자체가 영향을 미치기에 충분하다는 뜻에서) 단지 ~만의; 단지 ~에 불과한
You use mere to indicate that a quality or action that is usually unimportant has a very important or strong effect.

itch[복습]
[itʃ]

vi. 가렵다, 근질근질하다; n. 가려움
When a part of your body itches, you have an unpleasant feeling on your skin that makes you want to scratch.

prick one's ears

idiom 귀를 쫑긋 세우다
When an animal pricks their ears up, it raises or points them upward.

cock[*]
[kɔk]

v. (귀·꽁지를) 쫑긋 세우다, 위로 치올리다; n. 수탉; 마개
If you cock a part of your body in a particular direction, you lift it or point it in that direction.

grab[복습]
[græb]

v. 부여잡다, 움켜쥐다; n. 부여잡기
If you grab something, you take it or pick it up suddenly and roughly.

bony
[bóuni]

a. 뼈만 앙상한; 여윈
Someone who has a bony face or bony hands, for example, has a very thin face or very thin hands, with very little flesh covering their bones.

delicate[**]
[délikət]

a. 가냘픈, 여린; 섬세한, 고운; 예민한, 민감한
Something that is delicate is small and beautifully shaped.

skeleton＊
[skélətn]

n. 해골; 골격, 뼈대
Your skeleton is the framework of bones in your body.

exertion
[igzɔ́:rʃən]

n. 노력, 분투; 격심한 일, 고된 일
An exertion is using physical or mental energy, or hard work.

odd＊복습
[ad]

a. 이상한, 기묘한 (oddly ad. 묘하게, 이상하게)
If you describe someone or something as odd, you think that they
are strange or unusual.

breathless
[bréθlis]

a. 숨 가쁜, 숨도 못 쉴 정도의 (breathlessly ad. 숨이 차서, 헐떡이면서)
If you are breathless, you have difficulty in breathing properly, for
example because you have been running or because you are afraid
or excited.

skinny＊복습
[skíni]

a. 바짝 여윈, 깡마른
A skinny person is extremely thin, often in a way that you find
unattractive.

strike＊＊＊
[straik]

v. (struk–struk) 인상을 주다, ~이 생각나다; 치다, 찌르다; 습격하다; 충돌하다;
n. 공격, 공습; 파업
If something strikes you as being a particular thing, it gives you the
impression of being that thing.

overflow＊
[òuvərflóu]

v. 넘치다, 넘쳐흐르다; n. 넘쳐흐름, 범람
If a place or container is overflowing with people or things, it is too
full of them.

Chapters Fifteen & Sixteen

1. How did Sistine call her mother and why?
   A. She used a pay phone in front of the motel, because her cell phone battery had died.
   B. She used a pay phone in the laundry room, because Rob had no phone in his room.
   C. She used a phone in Rob's room, because it was the only phone they had.
   D. She used the phone at the main desk, because it was free.

2. What reason did Rob give his father for Sistine wearing his clothes?
   A. He said that her clothes had gotten wet in the rain.
   B. He said that her dress would make the tiger in the woods upset.
   C. He said that her dress was too pretty to wear in the woods.
   D. He said that she just wanted to wear them for fun.

3. What memory did Rob have that made the world seem full of light in contrast to life at the motel?
   A. A Christmas before his mother died when lights had been outside their home
   B. A Christmas after his mother died when his father took him to see a parade
   C. A Christmas before his mother died when they watched the stars together
   D. A Christmas after his mother died when his father bought a cake

4. Why is Sistine named Sistine?

  A. Her parents first met in a park called Sistine.

  B. Her parents had owned a puppy named Sistine.

  C. Her parents first met while looking at the ceiling in the Sistine Chapel.

  D. Her older brother had wanted a sister named Sistine.

5. Why was Rob not supposed to talk about his mother?

  A. It made Rob cry when he talked about her.

  B. It made his father cry whenever he said her name.

  C. The people in their own hometown were upset when Rob talked about her.

  D. She was gone and she wasn't coming back.

6. Why did Rob and his father move from Jacksonville to Lister?

  A. The people in Jacksonville always wanted to talk about Rob's mother.

  B. The people in Jacksonville stopped talking to Rob after Rob's mother died.

  C. Rob's father found a high paying job in Lister.

  D. Rob had family in Lister that they needed to visit.

7. How did Sistine's mother react to Sistine wearing Rob's clothes?

  A. She said Sistine looked like a boy.

  B. She said Sistine looked like a hobo.

  C. She said Sistine looked like a criminal.

  D. She said Sistine looked like a sick child.

Check Your Reading Speed

1분에 몇 단어를 읽는지 리딩 속도를 측정해보세요.

$$\frac{446 \text{ words}}{\text{reading time ( ) sec}} \times 60 = (\quad) \text{ WPM}$$

Build Your Vocabulary

make it^{복습}

idiom ~에 도착하다; (자기 분야에서) 성공하다
If you make it somewhere, you succeed in getting there, especially in time to do something.

parking lot
[páːrkiŋ lat]

n. 주차장
A parking lot is an area of ground where people can leave their cars.

barely*
[béərli]

ad. 간신히, 가까스로; 거의 ~없게
You use barely to say that something is only just true or only just the case.

seep
[siːp]

vi. 스며 나오다, 새다
If something such as liquid or gas seeps somewhere, it flows slowly and in small amounts into a place where it should not go.

squint
[skwint]

v. 실눈으로 보다, 곁눈질을 하다; a. 사시의; 곁눈질하는
If you squint at something, you look at it with your eyes partly closed.

laundry^{복습}
[lɔ́ːndri]

n. 세탁물; 세탁소 (laundry room n. 세탁실)
Laundry is used to refer to clothes, sheets, and towels that are about to be washed, are being washed, or have just been washed.

disbelief
[dìsbilíːf]

n. 불신, 믿지 않음
Disbelief is not believing that something is true or real.

change***
[tʃeindʒ]

n. 거스름돈, 잔돈; 변화, 변경; v. 변하다, 바꾸다
Change is coins, rather than paper money.

handful*
[hǽndfùl]

n. 한 움큼, 손에 그득, 한 줌
A handful of something is the amount of it that you can hold in your hand.

palm*
[paːm]

① n. 손바닥 ② n. [식물] 종려나무, 야자나무
The palm of your hand is the inside part.

trick^{복습}
[trik]

n. 묘기, 마술; 비결, 요령; v. 속이다; 장난치다
A trick is an action that is intended to deceive someone.

march^{복습}
[maːrtʃ]

① v. 당당하게 걷다, 행진하다; n. 행진, 행군 ② n. 3월
If you say that someone marches somewhere, you mean that they walk there quickly and in a determined way, for example because they are angry.

command[**] [kəmǽnd]

v. 명령하다, 지휘하다, 지배하다; n. 명령, 지휘

If someone in authority commands you to do something, they tell you that you must do it.

evaporate[*] [ivǽpərèit]

v. 사라지다; 증발시키다

If a feeling, plan, or activity evaporates, it gradually becomes weaker and eventually disappears completely.

cave[*] [keiv]

n. 동굴; v. 굴을 파다; 움푹 들어가다, 무너지다

A cave is a large hole in the side of a cliff or hill, or one that is under the ground.

light[**] [lait]

v. (lit/lighted–lit/lighted) 빛을 비추다; 불이 붙다, 불을 붙이다; n. 빛

If a place or object is lit by something, it has light shining on it.

string[**] [striŋ]

v. (strung–strung) 묶다, 매달다; n. 끈, 실; (악기의) 현[줄]

If you string something somewhere, you hang it up between two or more objects.

constellation [kànstəléiʃən]

n. [천문] 별자리, 성좌

A constellation is a group of stars which form a pattern and have a name.

scold[*] [skould]

v. 꾸짖다, 잔소리하다

If you scold someone, you speak angrily to them because they have done something wrong.

Check Your Reading Speed

1분에 몇 단어를 읽는지 리딩 속도를 측정해보세요.

$$\frac{908 \text{ words}}{\text{reading time ( ) sec}} \times 60 = (\qquad) \text{ WPM}$$

Build Your Vocabulary

curb*
[kə:rb]

n. (보도의) 연석; 재갈, 고삐; 구속; vt. 억제하다
The curb is the raised edge of a pavement or sidewalk which separates it from the road.

wrap**
[ræp]

v. 포장하다; 감싸다; n. 싸개, 덮개
When you wrap something, you fold paper or cloth tightly round it to cover it completely, for example in order to protect it or so that you can give it to someone as a present.

grocery
[gróusəri]

n. 식료 잡화점; (pl.) 식료 잡화류
A grocery or a grocery store is a grocer's shop.

neat**
[ni:t]

a. 산뜻한, 깔끔한; 뛰어난, 훌륭한 (neatly ad. 깔끔하게)
A neat place, thing, or person is tidy and smart, and has everything in the correct place.

turn out**
phrasal v. 결국은 ~이 되다, 결국은 ~임이 밝혀지다
That something turns out means it happens in a particular way or has a particular result.

task**
[tæsk]

n. 일, 직무, 과업
A task is an activity or piece of work which you have to do, usually as part of a larger project.

give up
phrasal v. 포기하다, 단념하다
If you give up, you decide that you cannot do something and stop trying to do it.

grease*
[gri:s]

n. 기름, 지방분; v. ~에 기름을 바르다[치다]
Grease is an oily substance.

stain*
[stein]

v. 얼룩지게 하다, 더러워지다; n. 얼룩, 오점
If a liquid stains something, the thing becomes colored or marked by the liquid.

relieve**
[rilí:v]

vt. (걱정·고통 등을) 덜다, 안도하게 하다, 완화하다
(relieved a. 안도하는, 다행으로 여기는)
If something relieves an unpleasant feeling or situation, it makes it less unpleasant or causes it to disappear completely.

shrug**
[ʃrʌg]

v. (어깨를) 으쓱하다; n. (양 손바닥을 내보이면서 어깨를) 으쓱하기
If you shrug, you raise your shoulders to show that you are not interested in something or that you do not know or care about something.

68

nod ^{복습}
[nɔd]

v. 끄덕이다, 끄덕여 표시하다; n. (동의·인사·신호·명령의) 끄덕임
If you nod, you move your head downward and upward to show agreement, understanding, or approval.

tilt *
[tilt]

v. (고개를) 기웃하다; 기울(이)다; n. 경사, 기울기
If you tilt part of your body, usually your head, you move it slightly upward or to one side.

shift *
[ʃift]

v. 옮기다, 이동하다; n. 교대 근무; 교체, 순환
If you shift something or if it shifts, it moves slightly.

patch *
[pætʃ]

n. (다른 것과 달라 보이는) 부분; 조각, 파편; 헝겊 조각; 반창고; v. 헝겊을 대고 깁다
A patch on a surface is a part of it which is different in appearance from the area around it.

shine ***
[ʃain]

v. (shone/shined–shone/shined) 빛나(게 하)다, 반짝이다; n. 빛, 빛남, 광채
When the sun or a light shines, it gives out bright light.

ceiling ^{복습}
[síːliŋ]

n. 천장
A ceiling is the horizontal surface that forms the top part or roof inside a room.

bump *
[bʌmp]

v. (쾅 하고) 부딪치다, 충돌하다; n. 충돌; 혹
If you bump into something or someone, you accidentally hit them while you are moving.

firework
[fáiərwɔ́ːrk]

n. 폭죽, 불꽃놀이
Firework is a small device containing powder that burns or explodes and produces bright colored lights and loud noises, used especially at celebrations.

sigh ^{복습}
[sai]

v. 한숨 쉬다; n. 한숨, 탄식
When you sigh, you let out a deep breath, as a way of expressing feelings such as disappointment, tiredness, or pleasure.

cancer *
[kǽnsər]

n. 암
Cancer is a serious disease in which cells in a person's body increase rapidly in an uncontrolled way, producing abnormal growths.

concentrate ^{복습}
[kánsəntrèit]

v. 집중하다, 전념하다
If you concentrate on something, you give all your attention to it.

suitcase ^{복습}
[súːtkèis]

n. 여행 가방
A suitcase is a box or bag with a handle and a hard frame in which you carry your clothes when you are traveling.

crunch
[krʌntʃ]

n. 저벅저벅 밟는 소리; v. 자박자박 밟고 가다; 우두둑 깨물다[부수다]
Crunch is a breaking or crushing noise, for example when you step on it.

gravel *
[grǽvəl]

n. 자갈; vt. 자갈로 덮다, ∼에 자갈을 깔다
Gravel consists of very small stones which is often used to make paths.

in time

idiom 때맞추어, 제시간에, 늦지 않고
If you do something in time, it means that you are not late to do it.

sweep^{복습}
[swi:p]

v. 휙 지나가다; 청소하다; 쓸어내리다, 휩쓸어 가다; (감정 등이) 엄습하다;
n. 한 번 휘두름; 청소
If something sweeps from one place to another, it moves there extremely quickly.

crack^{복습}
[kræk]

v. 금이 가다, 깨다; 날카로운 소리가 나게 하다; n. 날카로운 소리; 갈라진 금
If something hard cracks, or if you crack it, it becomes slightly damaged, with lines appearing on its surface.

slip^{복습}
[slip]

v. 미끄러지듯이 들어가다[움직이다], 미끄러지다; 재빨리 입다; 슬며시 두다
If something slips, it slides out of place or out of your hand.

businesslike
[bíznislàik]

a. 사무적인, 업무에 충실한
If you describe someone as businesslike, you mean that they deal with things in an efficient way without wasting time.

wobble
[wabl]

v. 흔들흔들하다, 비틀대다; 동요하다; n. 흔들림
If something or someone wobbles, they make small movements from side to side, for example because they are unsteady.

parking lot^{복습}
[pá:rkiŋ lat]

n. 주차장
A parking lot is an area of ground where people can leave their cars.

shade^{**}
[ʃeid]

n. 색조; 그늘, 음영; vt. 그늘지게 하다
A shade of a particular color is one of its different forms. For example, emerald green and olive green are shades of green.

pile^{**}
[pail]

v. 쌓아 올리다; 쌓이다; n. 쌓아 올린 더미; 다수
If you pile things somewhere, you put them there so that they form a pile.

profile[*]
[próufail]

n. 옆얼굴(의 윤곽), 측면; 외형, 윤곽
Your profile is the outline of your face as it is seen when someone is looking at you from the side.

chin^{복습}
[tʃin]

n. 아래턱, 턱 끝
Your chin is the part of your face that is below your mouth and above your neck.

pointed[*]
[pɔ́intid]

a. 뾰족한, 날카로운; (말·표현 등이) 예리한, 찌르는
Something that is pointed has a point at one end.

hobo
[hóubou]

n. 떠돌이 노동자, 부랑자; 떠돌이
A hobo is a worker, especially a farm worker, who goes from place to place in order to find work.

tap[*]
[tæp]

① v. 가볍게 두드리다; n. 가볍게 두드리기 ② n. 주둥이, (수도 등의) 꼭지
If you tap something, you hit it with a quick light blow or a series of quick light blows.

congressman[*]
[kɔ́ŋgresmən]

n. 미국 연방의회 의원, 하원 의원
A congressman is a male member of the US Congress, especially of the House of Representatives.

flick^{복습}
[flik]

vt. 잽싸게 움직이다; 가볍게 치다; 튀기다; n. 가볍게 치기
If something flicks in a particular direction, or if someone flicks it, it moves with a short, sudden movement.

70

mutter^{복습}
[mΛtər]

v. 중얼거리다, 불평하다; n. 중얼거림, 불평
If you mutter, you speak very quietly so that you cannot easily be heard, often because you are complaining about something.

growl^{복습}
[graul]

v. 으르렁거리다; n. 으르렁거리는 소리
If someone growls something, they say something in a low, rough, and angry voice.

throat^{복습}
[θrout]

n. 목(구멍)
Your throat is the back of your mouth and the top part of the tubes that go down into your stomach and your lungs.

stalk[*]
[stɔːk]

① vi. 활보하다, 화난 걸음으로[으스대며] 걷다; 몰래 접근하다 ② n. 줄기, 잎자루
If you stalk somewhere, you walk there in a stiff, proud, or angry way.

slam[*]
[slæm]

v. (문 따위를) 탕 닫다; 세게 치다; 털썩 내려놓다; n. 쾅 (하는 소리)
If you slam a door or window or if it slams, it shuts noisily and with great force.

pull away

phrasal v. (차가) 떠나다; (몸을) 빼다, 뿌리치다
When a vehicle pulls away, it begins to move.

slump
[slʌmp]

vi. 무너지듯이 앉다, 쿵 떨어지다; (기운 등이) 갑자기 없어지다; 폭락하다;
n. 슬럼프; 쿵 떨어짐
If you slump somewhere, you fall or sit down there heavily, for example because you are very tired or you feel ill.

whisper^{복습}
[hwíspəːr]

v. 속삭이다; n. 속삭임; 속삭이는 소리
When you whisper, you say something very quietly.

forbid[*]
[fərbíd]

vt. 금지하다, 허락하지 않다 (forbidden a. 금지된)
If you forbid someone to do something, or if you forbid an activity, you order that it must not be done.

1. Why did Rob want to get Willie May's opinion?
   A. He wanted to know if he should go back to school or not.
   B. He wanted to know if he should free the tiger or not.
   C. He wanted to know if he should date Sistine or not.
   D. He wanted to know if he should stay in Lister or not.

2. What had Willie May once owned?
   A. A green parakeet bird
   B. A green python snake
   C. A green chameleon
   D. A black and white cat

3. What had happened to Cricket?
   A. Willie May accidentally let him escape.
   B. Willie May gave him to a friend.
   C. He was eaten by a snake.
   D. Willie May let him go.

4. What memory came to Rob's mind as he thought of Cricket?

   A. He remembered his father giving him a bird as a child too.

   B. He remembered a bird that his mother used to own.

   C. He remembered his father shooting a bird.

   D. He remembered a time when he wanted a bird for his birthday.

5. Which of the following does NOT describe Beauchamp?

   A. He was the owner of the motel Kentucky Star.

   B. He was on the Kentucky Star's payroll.

   C. He was a large man with orange hair.

   D. He drove a red jeep.

6. What kind of deal did Beauchamp offer Rob?

   A. He offered to let Rob and his father stay at the motel for free.

   B. He offered to give Rob a ride to school in the mornings.

   C. He offered to let Rob show a wild animal to his friends from school.

   D. He offered to let Rob take care of a wild animal.

7. How did Beauchamp drive through the woods?

   A. He drove like he was crazy, swerving away from trees.

   B. He drove like he was a beginner, often driving in reverse.

   C. He drove very carefully and slowly through the woods.

   D. He drove at a normal speed down a dirt road through the woods.

Check Your Reading Speed

1분에 몇 단어를 읽는지 리딩 속도를 측정해보세요.

$$\frac{628 \text{ words}}{\text{reading time ( ) sec}} \times 60 = (\quad) \text{ WPM}$$

Build Your Vocabulary

chew
[tʃuː]

v. 씹다. 씹어서 으깨다
If you chew gum, you keep biting it and moving it around your mouth to taste the flavor of it.

toss *
[tɔːs]

v. 뒹굴다. 뒤척이다; 던지다. 내던지다; (머리 등을) 갑자기 쳐들다
If you toss and turn, you keep moving around in bed and cannot sleep properly, for example because you are ill or worried.

scratch
[skrætʃ]

v. 긁다; 할퀴다. 생채기를 내다; n. 긁기; 긁힌 자국. 긁는 소리
If you scratch yourself, you rub your fingernails against your skin because it is itching.

set free

phrasal v. (사람·동물을) 자유롭게 하다. 석방하다
If you set free someone or something, it means you grant freedom to them.

stink
[stiŋk]

v. (stank/stunk–stunk) 냄새가 나다. 구린내가 나다; 수상쩍다
To stink means to smell extremely unpleasant.

mind ***
[maind]

v. 싫어하다. 꺼리다; n. 마음. 정신
If you do not mind something, you are not annoyed or bothered by it.

snap *
[snæp]

v. ~을 탕 하고 열다[닫다]; 짤깍[툭] 소리 내다; 호되게 말하다; n. 짤깍 소리 냄
If you snap something into a particular position, or if it snaps into that position, it moves quickly into that position, with a sharp sound.

stare
[stɛər]

v. 응시하다. 뚫어지게 보다
If you stare at someone or something, you look at them for a long time.

palm
[paːm]

① n. 손바닥 ② n. [식물] 종려나무. 야자나무
The palm of your hand is the inside part.

drape
[dreip]

vt. 주름을 잡아 예쁘게 덮다; (손·발 등을) 되는 대로 걸치다; n. 드리워진 모양
If you drape a piece of cloth somewhere, you place it there so that it hangs down in a casual and graceful way.

cup ***
[kʌp]

vt. (손 등을) 잔 모양으로 만들다. 손을 모아 쥐다; n. 컵. 잔
If you cup something in your hands, you make your hands into a curved dish-like shape and support it or hold it gently.

entire
[intàiər]

a. 전체의; 완전한
You use entire when you want to emphasize that you are referring to the whole of something, for example, the whole of a place, time, or population.

beat ^{복습}
[biːt]

v. (심장이) 고동치다; 때리다, 치다, 두드리다; 패배시키다, 이기다; n. [음악] 박자
When your heart or pulse beats, it continually makes regular rhythmic movements.

cock ^{복습}
[kɔk]

v. (귀·꽁지를) 쫑긋 세우다, 위로 치올리다; n. 수탉; 마개
If you cock a part of your body in a particular direction, you lift it or point it in that direction.

on account of ^{복습}

idiom ~때문에, ~이므로
You use on account of to introduce the reason or explanation for something.

bend ^{복습}
[bend]

v. (bent–bent) 구부리다, 굽히다; 구부러지다, 휘다; n. 커브, 굽음
When you bend a part of your body such as your arm or leg, or when it bends, you change its position so that it is no longer straight.

pillow ^{복습}
[pílou]

n. 베개; 머리 받침대 (pillowcase n. 베갯잇, 베개 커버)
A pillow is a rectangular cushion which you rest your head on when you are in bed.

sink^{***}
[siŋk]

v. 가라앉다, 침몰하다
If your heart or your spirits sink, you become depressed or lose hope.

stand^{***}
[stænd]

vi. 참다, 견디다; 서다, 일어서다; n. 가판대, 좌판; 관람석
If you cannot stand something, you cannot bear it or tolerate it.

favor^{***}
[féivər]

n. 호의, 친절
If you do someone a favor, you do something for them even though you do not have to.

supper ^{복습}
[sʌ́pər]

n. 저녁 식사, (가벼운) 만찬
Supper is a simple meal eaten just before you go to bed at night.

flit
[flit]

vi. 휙휙[훨훨] 날다, 날아다니다; 스쳐가다
If something such as a bird or a bat flits about, it flies quickly from one place to another.

grab ^{복습}
[græb]

v. 부여잡다, 움켜쥐다; n. 부여잡기
If you grab something, you take it or pick it up suddenly and roughly.

billow
[bílou]

vi. (바람에) 부풀어 오르다; (연기·구름이) 피어오르다
When something made of cloth billows, it swells out and moves slowly in the wind.

aim^{***}
[eim]

n. 겨냥, 조준; 목적, 뜻; v. 겨냥을 하다, 목표삼다; ~할 작정이다
Your aim is your skill or action in pointing a weapon or other object at its target.

suspend[*]
[səspénd]

v. 매달다, 걸다; 중지하다
If something is suspended from a high place, it is hanging from that place.

midair
[midéər]

n. 공중, 중천
If something happens in midair, it happens in the air, rather than on the ground.

pin^{**}
[pin]

vt. ~을 꼼짝 못하게 누르다; 핀으로 꽂다, 고정하다; n. 핀, 장식

If someone pins you to something, they press you against a surface so that you cannot move.

bullet^{**}
[búlit]

n. (소총·권총의) 총탄, 탄환

A bullet is a small piece of metal with a pointed or rounded end, which is fired out of a gun.

thud^{복습}
[θʌd]

n. 쿵, 털썩(무거운 물건이 떨어지는 소리); v. (둔탁한 소리를 내며) 쿵 떨어지다

A thud is a dull sound, such as that a heavy object makes when it hits something soft.

76

Check Your Reading Speed

1분에 몇 단어를 읽는지 리딩 속도를 측정해보세요.

$$\frac{635 \text{ words}}{\text{reading time ( ) sec}} \times 60 = (\quad) \text{ WPM}$$

Build Your Vocabulary

sweep [swi:p]
v. 청소하다; 쓸어내리다, 휩쓸어 가다; 휙 지나가다; (감정 등이) 엄습하다;
n. 한 번 휘두름; 청소
If you sweep an area of floor or ground, you push dirt or rubbish off it using a brush with a long handle.

walkway [wɔ́:kwei]
n. 통로, 작은 길
A walkway is a passage or path for people to walk along. Walkways are often raised above the ground.

pull up
phrasal v. 차를 세우다, (말·차 등이) 서다
When a vehicle or driver pulls up, the vehicle slows down and stops.

honk [hɔ:ŋk]
v. 경적을 울리다; (거위·기러기가) 울다
If you honk the horn of a vehicle or if the horn honks, you make the horn produce a short loud sound.

horn [hɔ:rn]
n. (자동차 등의) 경적; 뿔
On a vehicle such as a car, the horn is the device that makes a loud noise as a signal or warning.

holler [hálər]
v. 큰 소리로 부르다; 고함지르다; n. 외침, 큰 소리
If you holler, you shout loudly.

beard [biərd]
n. (턱)수염
A man's beard is the hair that grows on his chin and cheeks.

permanent [pɔ́:rmənənt]
a. 영구적인, 변하지 않는
Something that is permanent lasts forever.

toothpick [tú:θpik]
n. 이쑤시개
A toothpick is a small stick which you use to remove food from between your teeth.

waggle [wǽgl]
v. 흔들(리)다, 좌우로 움직이다
If you waggle something, or if something waggles, it moves up and down or from side to side with short quick movements.

hoot [hu:t]
v. 야유하다, 콧방귀 끼다; 경적을 울리다; (올빼미 등이) 울다;
n. 외침소리, 폭소; 올빼미 울음소리
If you hoot, you make a loud high-pitched noise when you are laughing or showing disapproval.

hop [hap]
v. 깡충 뛰다, 뛰어오르다; n. 깡충깡충 뜀
If you hop, you move along by jumping.

Chapter Eighteen

77

graduate**
[grǽdʒueit]

vi. 졸업하다
When a student graduates, they complete their studies successfully and leave their school or university.

bury^{복습}
[béri]

vt. 묻다, 파묻다, 매장하다
If something buries itself somewhere, or if you bury it there, it is pushed very deeply in there.

wink*
[wiŋk]

v. 반짝거리다, 깜박이다; 윙크[눈짓]하다
When a light winks, it flashes on and off.

slap^{복습}
[slæp]

v. 찰싹 때리다; 탁 놓다; n. 찰싹 (때림)
If you slap someone, you hit them with the palm of your hand.

jerk^{복습}
[dʒə:rk]

① v. 갑자기 움직이다; n. 갑자기 움직임; 반사 운동 ② n. 바보, 멍청이
If you jerk something or someone in a particular direction, or they jerk in a particular direction, they move a short distance very suddenly and quickly.

handle**
[hǽndl]

vt. 다루다, 처리하다; 대다; n. 손잡이, 핸들
If you say that someone can handle a problem or situation, you mean that they have the ability to deal with it successfully.

spending money
[spéndiŋ mʌ́ni]

n. 용돈
Spending money is money that you have or are given to spend on personal things for pleasure, especially when you are on holiday.

skip*
[skip]

v. 깡충깡충 뛰다, 뛰어다니다; 건너뛰다, 생략하다
If you skip along, you move almost as if you are dancing, with a series of little jumps from one foot to the other.

property**
[prápərti]

n. 재산, 자산; 성질, 특성
Someone's property is all the things that belong to them or something that belongs to them.

in the meantime^{복습}

idiom 그 동안에
In the meantime or meantime means in the period of time between two events.

maintenance^{복습}
[méintənəns]

n. 관리, 유지, 점검
The maintenance of a building, vehicle, road, or machine is the process of keeping it in good condition by regularly checking it and repairing it when necessary.

broom^{복습}
[bru:m]

n. 빗자루, 비
A broom is a kind of brush with a long handle. You use a broom for sweeping the floor.

fervent
[fə́:rvənt]

a. 열렬한, 열심인; 뜨거운, 불타는 (fervently ad. 열렬하게, 열심히)
A fervent person has or shows strong feelings about something, and is very sincere and enthusiastic about it.

passenger**
[pǽsəndʒər]

n. 승객, 여객 (passenger seat n. 조수석)
A passenger in a vehicle such as a bus, boat, or plane is a person who is traveling in it, but who is not driving it or working on it.

grocery^{복습}
[gróusəri]

n. 식료 잡화점; (pl.) 식료 잡화류
A grocery or a grocery store is a grocer's shop.

78

swing ^{복습}
[swiŋ]

v. (swung—swung) 빙 돌다, 돌리다; 흔들(리)다
If something swings in a particular direction or if you swing it in that direction, it moves in that direction with a smooth, curving movement.

stink ^{복습}
[stiŋk]

v. (stank/stunk—stunk) 냄새가 나다, 구린내가 나다; 수상쩍다
To stink means to smell extremely unpleasant.

crank
[kræŋk]

v. 크랭크를 돌려 시동시키다; n. 크랭크
If you crank an engine or machine, you make it move or function, especially by turning a handle.

roar ^{복습}
[rɔ:r]

vi. (기계 등이) 큰 소리 내며 움직이다; (큰 짐승 등이) 으르렁거리다, 고함치다;
n. 외치는 소리, 왁자지껄함; 으르렁거리는 소리
If something, usually a vehicle, roars somewhere, it goes there very fast, making a loud noise.

tear ^{복습}
[tɛər]

① v. 부리나케 가다; 찢다, 찢어지다; n. 찢음 ② n. 눈물
If you tear somewhere, you move there very quickly, often in an uncontrolled or dangerous way.

gun ^{***}
[gʌn]

v. 속도를 갑자기 올리다; 총으로 쏘다; n. 총, 대포
To gun an engine or a vehicle means to make it start or go faster by pressing on the accelerator pedal.

swerve
[swə:rv]

v. 휙 방향을 틀다, 벗어나다, 빗나가다; n. 벗어남, 빗나감
If a vehicle or other moving thing swerves or if you swerve it, it suddenly changes direction, often in order to avoid hitting something.

whoop
[hup]

v. (열광·흥분 등으로) 환호성을 지르다; n. 함성, 환성
If you whoop, you shout loudly in a very happy or excited way.

Chapters Nineteen & Twenty

1. How had Beauchamp come to own the tiger?
   A. Beauchamp bought the tiger from a zoo about to close down.
   B. Someone had given him a tiger as a birthday present.
   C. Someone had owed him money and paid him with a tiger.
   D. Beauchamp traveled to India, found the tiger, and brought it home.

2. What did Beauchamp give Rob to help him with his new job?
   A. He gave him gloves to wear when handling the meat.
   B. He gave him key to the refrigerator where he kept the meat.
   C. He gave him keys to the jeep.
   D. He gave him keys to the tiger's cage.

3. How did Beauchamp seem after feeding the tiger?
   A. He seemed confidently as if he had done it many times.
   B. He seemed fearlessly as if he were stronger than the tiger.
   C. He seemed scared, sweating and with hands trembling.
   D. He seemed annoyed, sighing and looking bored.

4. What did the tiger do that reminded Rob of Sistine?
   A. He stared with a fierce look in his eyes.
   B. He roared as if he were upset.
   C. He paced back and forth.
   D. He ate as if he were starving.

5. What was Rob dismayed to see Sistine wearing when she came to the motel?
   A. The same pink dress from the first day they met
   B. His shirt and jeans from the previous day
   C. A T-shirt with a tiger on it
   D. A clean and neat school uniform

6. After reading the book on big cats, what did Sistine suggest for the tiger?
   A. She suggested that he could become tamed like a pet.
   B. She suggested that he would be happier in the cage after all.
   C. She suggested that he could help Rob hunt for food in the woods.
   D. She suggested that he could live with the panthers in the woods.

7. How did Rob react when Sistine started crying?
   A. He put his palm on her neck and whispered the same words his mother told him.
   B. He tried to ignore her crying because he refused to cry himself.
   C. He called her a real sissy and walked away from her.
   D. He thought of his mother and began to cry too.

Check Your Reading Speed

1분에 몇 단어를 읽는지 리딩 속도를 측정해보세요.

$$\frac{786 \text{ words}}{\text{reading time ( ) sec}} \times 60 = (\quad) \text{ WPM}$$

Build Your Vocabulary

cheat**
[tʃiːt]
v. 속이다; 규칙을 어기다; n. 사기
When someone cheats, they do not obey a set of rules which they should be obeying, for example in a game or exam.

pull up^{복습}
phrasal v. 차를 세우다, (말·차 등이) 서다
When a vehicle or driver pulls up, the vehicle slows down and stops.

crow
[krou]
① vi. 의기양양해 하다; (수탉이) 울다; n. 수탉의 울음소리 ② n. 까마귀
If you say that someone is crowing about something they have achieved or are pleased about, you disapprove of them because they keep telling people proudly about it.

amaze^{복습}
[əméiz]
vt. 깜짝 놀라게 하다 (amazed a. 놀란)
If something amazes you, it surprises you very much.

fellow**
[félou]
n. 녀석, 친구; 동료; a. 같은 처지에 있는, 동료의
A fellow is a man or boy.

owe**
[ou]
vt. 은혜를 입고 있다, 빚지고 있다
If you owe money to someone, they have lent it to you and you have not yet paid it back.

toothpick^{복습}
[túːθpìk]
n. 이쑤시개
A toothpick is a small stick which you use to remove food from between your teeth.

steady**
[stédi]
vt. 흔들리지 않게 하다, 안정시키다; a. 한결같은, 고른; 확고한
If you steady something or if it steadies, it stops shaking or moving about.

figure***
[fígjər]
v. 생각하다, 판단하다, 계산하다; n. 형태, 형상; 수치, 숫자; 작은 조각상
If you figure that something is the case, you think or guess that it is the case.

tap^{복습}
[tæp]
① v. 가볍게 두드리다; n. 가볍게 두드리기 ② n. 주둥이, (수도 등의) 꼭지
If you tap something, you hit it with a quick light blow or a series of quick light blows.

skin***
[skin]
v. 껍질을 벗기다; 생채기 내다, 스쳐서 상처를 입히다; n. 피부; 가죽
If you skin a dead animal, you remove its skin.

feed**
[fiːd]
v. 음식[먹이]을 주다, 먹이다; 공급하다; n. 먹이, 사료
If you feed a person or animal, you give them food to eat and sometimes actually put it in their mouths.

swallow**
[swálou]

v. (초조해서) 마른침을 삼키다; 삼키다. 목구멍으로 넘기다
If you swallow, you make a movement in your throat as if you are swallowing something, often because you are nervous or frightened.

dig**
[dig]

v. (dug–dug) 파헤치다, 파다; 찌르다; n. 파기
If you dig into something such as a deep container, you put your hand in it to search for something.

jingle
[dʒiŋgl]

n. 딸랑딸랑 울리는 소리; v. 짤랑짤랑 소리를 내다
When something jingles or when you jingle it, it makes a gentle ringing noise, like small bells.

attention**
[əténʃən]

n. 주의, 관심; 배려
If you pay attention to someone, you watch them, listen to them, or take notice of them.

terrify*
[térəfài]

vt. 무섭게[겁나게] 하다; 놀래다 (terrified a. 겁먹은, 무서워하는)
If something terrifies you, it makes you feel extremely frightened.

exist***
[igzíst]

v. 존재하다; 살아가다
If something exists, it is present in the world as a real thing.

nod^{복습}
[nɔd]

v. 끄덕이다, 끄덕여 표시하다; n. (동의·인사·신호·명령의) 끄덕임
If you nod, you move your head downward and upward to show agreement, understanding, or approval.

toss^{복습}
[tɔːs]

v. 던지다, 내던지다; (머리 등을) 갑자기 쳐들다; 뒹굴다, 뒤척이다
If you toss something somewhere, you throw it there lightly, often in a rather careless way.

swing^{복습}
[swiŋ]

v. (swung–swung) 빙 돌다, 돌리다; 흔들(리)다
If something swings in a particular direction or if you swing it in that direction, it moves in that direction with a smooth, curving movement.

grunt*
[grʌnt]

n. 꿀꿀[툴툴]거리는 소리; vi. (사람이) 툴툴거리다; (돼지가) 꿀꿀거리다
Grunt is a low sound you made when you are annoyed or not interested in something.

grocery^{복습}
[gróusəri]

n. 식료 잡화점; (pl.) 식료 잡화류
A grocery or a grocery store is a grocer's shop.

leap*
[liːp]

v. 껑충 뛰다; 뛰어넘다; n. 뜀, 도약
If you leap, you jump high in the air or jump a long distance.

stumble*
[stʌmbl]

v. 비틀거리며 걷다, 발부리가 걸리다; n. 비틀거림
If you stumble, you put your foot down awkwardly while you are walking or running and nearly fall over.

straighten^{복습}
[streitn]

v. 똑바르게 하다; 곧게 하다
If you straighten something, you make it tidy or put it in its proper position.

forehead^{복습}
[fɔ́ːrhèd]

n. 이마
Your forehead is the area at the front of your head between your eyebrows and your hair.

sweat^{복습}
[swet]

n. 땀; v. 땀 흘리다; 습기가 차다
Sweat is the salty colorless liquid which comes through your skin when you are hot, ill, or afraid.

tremble^{복습}
[trembl]

v. (공포·추위·피로 등으로) 떨(리)다; 흔들리다; n. 떨림; 진동
If something trembles, it shakes slightly.

shrug^{복습}
[ʃrʌg]

v. (어깨를) 으쓱하다; n. (양 손바닥을 내보이면서 어깨를) 으쓱하기
If you shrug, you raise your shoulders to show that you are not interested in something or that you do not know or care about something.

blush[*]
[blʌʃ]

v. 얼굴을 붉히다. (얼굴이) 빨개지다; n. 얼굴을 붉힘. 홍조
When you blush, your face becomes redder than usual because you are ashamed or embarrassed.

sweaty
[swéti]

a. (사람·몸·옷 등이) 땀이 나는. 땀투성이의
If parts of your body or your clothes are sweaty, they are soaked or covered with sweat.

mock[*]
[mak]

vt. 흉내 내며 놀리다. 조롱하다; n. 조롱. 놀림감; a. 가짜의. 모의의
(mocking a. 조롱하는)
You use mock to describe something which is not real or genuine, but which is intended to be very similar to the real thing.

grab^{복습}
[græb]

v. 부여잡다. 움켜쥐다; n. 부여잡기
If you grab something, you take it or pick it up suddenly and roughly.

muzzle
[mʌzl]

n. (동물의) 주둥이. 부리; 총구. 포구; vt. 재갈 물리다. 말 못하게 하다
The muzzle of an animal such as a dog is its nose and mouth.

fierce^{복습}
[fiərs]

a. 사나운; 격렬한. 지독한
A fierce animal or person is very aggressive or angry.

tatter^{복습}
[tǽtər]

v. 해지다; 갈가리 찢다; n. 넝마. 누더기 옷 (tattered a. 해진)
If something such as clothing or a book is tattered, it is damaged or torn, especially because it has been used a lot over a long period of time.

remind^{복습}
[rimáind]

vt. 생각나게 하다. 상기시키다. 일깨우다
If someone reminds you of a fact or event that you already know about, they say something which makes you think about it.

glow^{복습}
[glou]

v. 빛을 내다. 빛나다; n. 빛. 밝음
If something glows, it produces a dull, steady light.

insist^{**}
[insíst]

v. 우기다. 주장하다; 강요하다
If you insist that something is the case, you say so very firmly and refuse to say otherwise, even though other people do not believe you.

Check Your Reading Speed

1분에 몇 단어를 읽는지 리딩 속도를 측정해보세요.

$$\frac{800 \text{ words}}{\text{reading time ( ) sec}} \times 60 = (\quad) \text{ WPM}$$

Build Your Vocabulary

concern**
[kənsə́:rn]

vt. ~에 관계하다; 염려하다; 관심을 갖다; n. 염려; 관심
If a situation, event, or activity concerns you, it affects or involves you.

in the meantime^{복습}

idiom 그 동안에
In the meantime or meantime means in the period of time between two events.

pull up^{복습}

phrasal v. 차를 세우다, (말·차 등이) 서다
When a vehicle or driver pulls up, the vehicle slows down and stops.

belch*
[beltʃ]

v. 분출하다, 내뿜다; 트림을 하다; n. 트림 (소리); 폭발(음), 분출
If a machine or chimney belches something such as smoke or fire or if smoke or fire belches from it, large amounts of smoke or fire come from it.

gasp^{복습}
[gæsp]

v. (놀람 따위로) 숨이 막히다, 헐떡거리다; n. 헐떡거림
When you gasp, you take a short quick breath through your mouth, especially when you are surprised, shocked, or in pain.

sigh^{복습}
[sai]

v. 한숨 쉬다; n. 한숨, 탄식
When you sigh, you let out a deep breath, as a way of expressing feelings such as disappointment, tiredness, or pleasure.

pelt
[pelt]

vt. 내던지다, 연타하다, 퍼붓다
If you pelt someone with things, you throw things at them.

dodge*
[dadʒ]

v. (재빨리) 피하다, 몸을 홱 피하다; n. 발뺌
If you dodge something, you avoid it by quickly moving aside or out of reach so that it cannot hit or reach you.

battlefield
[bǽtlfi:ld]

n. 싸움터, 전장
A battlefield is a place where a battle is fought.

dismay*
[disméi]

vt. 깜짝 놀라게 하다, 당황하게 하다; n. 실망, 낙담, 경악 (dismayed a. 깜짝 놀란)
If you are dismayed by something, it makes you feel afraid, worried, or sad.

blurt
[blə:rt]

vt. 불쑥 말하다; 무심결에 누설하다
If someone blurts something, they say it suddenly, after trying hard to keep quiet or to keep it secret.

grocery^{복습}
[gróusəri]

n. 식료 잡화점; (pl.) 식료 잡화류
A grocery or a grocery store is a grocer's shop.

set free^{복습}
phrasal v. (사람·동물을) 자유롭게 하다, 석방하다
If you set free someone or something, it means you grant freedom to them.

bump^{복습}
[bʌmp]
v. (쾅 하고) 부딪치다, 충돌하다; n. 충돌; 혹
If you bump against something or someone, you accidentally hit them while you are moving.

beat^{복습}
[biːt]
v. 패배시키다, 이기다; 때리다, 치다, 두드리다; (심장이) 고동치다; n. [음악] 박자
If you beat someone in a competition or election, you defeat them.

press^{**}
[pres]
v. 누르다, 밀어 누르다; 강요하다; n. 누름, 압박; 언론, 출판물
If you press something or press down on it, you push hard against it with your foot or hand.

wrap^{복습}
[ræp]
v. 감싸다; 포장하다; n. 싸개, 덮개
If someone wraps their arms, fingers, or legs around something, they put them firmly around it.

endanger
[indéindʒər]
v. ~을 위험에 빠뜨리다, 위태롭게 하다 (endangered a. 위험에 빠진)
To endanger something or someone means to put them in a situation where they might be harmed or destroyed completely.

species[*]
[spíːʃiːz]
n. 종, 종류
A species is a class of plants or animals whose members have the same main characteristics and are able to breed with each other.

watch out
idiom 조심해라!
You say 'watch out,' when you warn someone about something dangerous.

desperate^{복습}
[déspərit]
a. 필사적인; 자포자기의, 절망적인 (desperately ad. 필사적으로)
If you are desperate for something or desperate to do something, you want or need it very much indeed.

skinny^{복습}
[skíni]
a. 바싹 여윈, 깡마른
A skinny person is extremely thin, often in a way that you find unattractive.

starve^{복습}
[staːrv]
v. 굶주리다, 굶어죽다
If people starve, they suffer greatly from lack of food which sometimes leads to their death.

suitcase^{복습}
[súːtkèis]
n. 여행 가방
A suitcase is a box or bag with a handle and a hard frame in which you carry your clothes when you are traveling.

throat^{복습}
[θrout]
n. 목(구멍) (clear one's throat idiom 목을 가다듬다)
Your throat is the back of your mouth and the top part of the tubes that go down into your stomach and your lungs.

hire[*]
[haiər]
vt. 고용하다; 빌리다, 빌려주다; n. 고용
If you hire someone, you employ them or pay them to do a particular job for you.

feed^{복습}
[fiːd]
v. 음식[먹이]을 주다, 먹이다; 공급하다; n. 먹이, 사료
If you feed a person or animal, you give them food to eat and sometimes actually put it in their mouths.

make sense

idiom 뜻이 통하다, 도리에 맞다; 이해하다, 뜻을 알다
If something makes sense, it has a meaning that you can easily understand.

saw^{복습}
[sɔ:]

① vt. 톱으로 자르다; n. 톱 ② v. SEE의 과거·과거분사형
If you saw something, you cut it with a saw.

mock^{복습}
[mak]

vt. 흉내 내며 놀리다, 조롱하다; n. 조롱, 놀림감; a. 가짜의, 모의의
You use mock to describe something which is not real or genuine, but which is intended to be very similar to the real thing.

spin^{**}
[spin]

v. (spun−spun) 돌리다, 맴돌리다; 오래[질질] 끌다; n. 회전
If something spins or if you spin it, it turns quickly around a central point.

pace^{복습}
[peis]

v. 왔다 갔다 하다, 천천히 걷다; n. 걸음걸이; 속도
If you pace a small area, you keep walking up and down it, because you are anxious or impatient.

rattle[*]
[rætl]

v. 왈각달각 소리 나(게 하)다, 덜컹덜컹 움직이(게 하)다; 재잘거리다;
n. 덜거덕거리는 소리
When something rattles or when you rattle it, it makes short sharp knocking sounds because it is being shaken or it keeps hitting against something hard.

choke^{**}
[tʃouk]

v. 숨이 막히다, 질식시키다; n. 질식
When you choke or when something chokes you, you cannot breathe properly or get enough air into your lungs.

terrify^{복습}
[térəfài]

vt. 무섭게[겁나게] 하다; 놀래다 (terrified a. 겁먹은, 무서워하는)
If something terrifies you, it makes you feel extremely frightened.

comfort^{**}
[kʌ́mfərt]

vt. 위로[위안]하다, 안심시키다; n. 마음이 편안함, 안락; 위로, 위안
If you comfort someone, you make them feel less worried, unhappy, or upset, for example by saying kind things to them.

cup^{복습}
[kʌp]

vt. (손 등을) 잔 모양으로 만들다, 손을 모아 쥐다; n. 컵, 잔
If you cup something in your hands, you make your hands into a curved dish-like shape and support it or hold it gently.

palm^{복습}
[pa:m]

① n. 손바닥 ② n. [식물] 종려나무, 야자나무
The palm of your hand is the inside part.

pulse[*]
[pʌls]

n. 맥박, 고동; 파동; v. 고동치다, 맥이 뛰다
Your pulse is the regular beating of blood through your body, which you can feel when you touch particular parts of your body, especially your wrist.

in time^{복습}

idiom 제시간에, 늦지 않고, 때맞추어
If you do something in time, it means that you are not late to do it.

whisper^{복습}
[hwíspə:r]

v. 속삭이다; n. 속삭임; 속삭이는 소리
When you whisper, you say something very quietly.

1. How did Willie May feel about Sistine when they first met?
   A. She thought Sistine was angry.
   B. She thought Sistine was annoying.
   C. She thought Sistine was clever.
   D. She thought Sistine was rude.

2. What advice did Willie May give Sistine?
   A. Let the anger rise from her legs to reach her heart.
   B. Somebody was coming to rescue her if she waited a little longer.
   C. Nobody was going to rescue her so she had to rescue herself.
   D. She could rescue herself if she used her anger wisely.

3. What did Sistine think of Willie May?
   A. She thought she was a psychopath, someone who was crazy.
   B. She thought she was a psychic, someone who could read minds.
   C. She thought she was a professional, someone very talented.
   D. She thought she was a prophetess, a woman who God speaks through.

4. What did Rob's father think of the meat in the motel room?
   A. He was angry that Beauchamp would put Rob in danger near a tiger.
   B. He was grateful because he thought Beauchamp was helping his family.
   C. He was upset because he thought Beauchamp was insulting him and his family.
   D. He was annoyed that Rob let it rot in the heat.

5. What did Rob's father do at the gun case?
   A. He walked to the gun case but then just turned around quickly.
   B. He just stood there and stared at the gun.
   C. He unlocked it and grabbed the gun.
   D. He unlocked it but just looked at the gun.

6. What did Rob carve from the wood as he recalled a memory under a big oak tree?
   A. A big oak leaf
   B. A bird's egg
   C. A hunting rifle
   D. Willie May's Cricket

Check Your Reading Speed

1분에 몇 단어를 읽는지 리딩 속도를 측정해보세요.

$$\frac{661 \text{ words}}{\text{reading time (} \quad \text{) sec}} \times 60 = (\quad) \text{ WPM}$$

Build Your Vocabulary

dusk[*]
[dʌsk]

n. 해질녘, 황혼
Dusk is the time just before night when the daylight has almost gone but when it is not completely dark.

parking lot[복습]
[páːrkiŋ lat]

n. 주차장
A parking lot is an area of ground where people can leave their cars.

laundry[복습]
[lɔ́ːndri]

n. 세탁물; 세탁소 (laundry room n. 세탁실)
Laundry is used to refer to clothes, sheets, and towels that are about to be washed, are being washed, or have just been washed.

materialize
[mətíəriəlàiz]

v. 나타나다; ~에 형체를 부여하다, 구체화[실현]하다
If a person or thing materializes, they suddenly appear, after they have been invisible or in another place.

lean[복습]
[liːn]

① v. 기대다, 의지하다; 몸을 구부리다, 기울다 ② a. 야윈, 마른
If you lean on or against someone or something, you rest against them so that they partly support your weight.

cigarette[복습]
[sigərét]

n. 담배
Cigarettes are small tubes of paper containing tobacco which people smoke.

jerk[복습]
[dʒəːrk]

① v. 갑자기 움직이다; n. 갑자기 움직임; 반사 운동 ② n. 바보, 멍청이
If you jerk something or someone in a particular direction, or they jerk in a particular direction, they move a short distance very suddenly and quickly.

wink[복습]
[wiŋk]

v. 반짝거리다, 깜박이다; 윙크[눈짓]하다
When a light winks, it flashes on and off.

hang around

phrasal v. 서성거리다, 배회하다
If you hang around somewhere, you spend time there without doing very much.

scare[**]
[skɛəːr]

v. 위협하다, 겁나게 하다
If something scares you, it frightens or worries you.

mean[**]
[miːn]

① a. 비열한; 성질이 나쁜, 심술궂은 ② vt. 의미하다, 뜻하다 ③ a. 평균의, 중간의
If you describe a behavior as mean, you are saying that it is very bad and evil.

90

snap ^{복습}
[snæp]

v. 날카롭게[느닷없이] 말하다; ~을 탕 하고 열다[닫다]; 짤깍[툭] 소리 내다;
n. 짤깍 소리 냄
If someone snaps at you, they speak to you in a sharp, unfriendly way.

stick ^{복습}
[stik]

① n. 막대기, 지팡이 ② v. 내밀다; 찔러 넣다, 찌르다; 달라붙다, 붙이다; 고수하다
A stick of something is a long thin piece of it.

stare ^{복습}
[stɛər]

v. 응시하다, 뚫어지게 보다
If you stare at someone or something, you look at them for a long time.

desperate ^{복습}
[déspərit]

a. 필사적인; 자포자기의, 절망적인 (desperately ad. 필사적으로)
If you are desperate for something or desperate to do something, you want or need it very much indeed.

nod ^{복습}
[nɔd]

v. 끄덕이다, 끄덕여 표시하다; n. (동의·인사·신호·명령의) 끄덕임
If you nod, you move your head downward and upward to show agreement, understanding, or approval.

extend ^{복습}
[iksténd]

v. 주다, 베풀다; (손·발 등을) 뻗다, 늘이다; 넓히다, 확장하다
If you extend something to other people or things, you make it include or affect more people or things.

light ^{복습}
[lait]

v. (lit/lighted–lit/lighted) 불을 붙이다, 불이 붙다; 빛을 비추다; n. 빛
If you light something such as a cigarette or fire, or if it lights, it starts burning.

sorrow [*]
[sárou]

n. 슬픔, 비통; 후회
Sorrow is a feeling of deep sadness or regret.

lightning [*]
[láitniŋ]

n. 번개, 번갯불
Lightning is the very bright flashes of light in the sky that happen during thunderstorms.

pair ^{**}
[pɛər]

n. 한 쌍[켤레]; (쌍을 이룬 것의) 한 쪽; v. 짝을 짓다, 쌍으로 하다
You can refer to two people as a pair when they are standing or walking together or when they have some kind of relationship with each other.

stretch ^{복습}
[stretʃ]

v. 쭉 펴다, 뻗다, 늘이다; n. (특히 길게 뻗은) 길, 구간; 뻗침
When you stretch, you put your arms or legs out straight and tighten your muscles.

straighten ^{복습}
[streitn]

v. 똑바르게 하다, 곧게 하다
If you straighten something, you make it tidy or put it in its proper position.

rescue [*]
[réskjuː]

vt. 구조하다, 구출하다; n. 구출, 구원
If you rescue someone, you get them out of a dangerous or unpleasant situation.

crank ^{복습}
[kræŋk]

v. 크랭크를 돌려 시동시키다; n. 크랭크
If you crank an engine or machine, you make it move or function, especially by turning a handle.

prophetess
[práfitis]

n. 여자 예언자

A prophetess is a female who is believed to be chosen by God to say the things that God wants to tell people.

ceiling 복습
[síːliŋ]

n. 천장

A ceiling is the horizontal surface that forms the top part or roof inside a room.

make sense 복습

idiom 뜻이 통하다, 도리에 맞다; 이해하다, 뜻을 알다

If something makes sense, it has a meaning that you can easily understand.

Check Your Reading Speed

1분에 몇 단어를 읽는지 리딩 속도를 측정해보세요.

$$\frac{792 \text{ words}}{\text{reading time (} \quad \text{) sec}} \times 60 = (\quad) \text{ WPM}$$

Build Your Vocabulary

sink ^{복습}
[siŋk]

v. (sank–sunk) 가라앉다, 침몰하다
If your heart or your spirits sink, you become depressed or lose hope.

feed ^{복습}
[fi:d]

v. 음식[먹이]을 주다, 먹이다; 공급하다; n. 먹이, 사료
If you feed a person or animal, you give them food to eat and sometimes actually put it in their mouths.

hardly ^{***}
[háːrdli]

ad. 거의 ~아니다, 조금도 ~않다
When you say you can hardly do something, you are emphasizing that it is very difficult for you to do it.

get by

phrasal v. (곤란을 극복하고) 그럭저럭 헤어나다, 살아남다; (검열 등을) 통과하다
To get by means to manage to live or do a particular thing using the money, knowledge, or equipment that you have in spite of difficulties.

rot ^{복습}
[rat]

v. 썩다, 썩이다; n. 썩음, 부패 (rotten a. 썩은, 부패한)
When food, wood, or another substance rots, or when something rots it, it becomes softer and is gradually destroyed.

hold one's tongue

idiom 잠자코 있다, 침묵을 지키다
When you hold your tongue, you remain silent although you would like to give your opinion.

twig [*]
[twig]

n. 잔가지, 가는 가지
A twig is a very small thin branch that grows out from a main branch of a tree or bush.

crack ^{복습}
[kræk]

v. 날카로운 소리가 나게 하다; 금이 가다, 깨다; n. 날카로운 소리; 갈라진 금
If something cracks, or if you crack it, it makes a sharp sound like the sound of a piece of wood breaking.

knuckle ^{복습}
[nʌkl]

n. 손가락 관절[마디]; v. 손가락 마디로 치다
Your knuckles are the rounded pieces of bone that form lumps on your hands where your fingers join your hands, and where your fingers bend.

reproachful
[ripróutʃfəl]

a. 나무라는, 책망하는, 비난하는 (듯한)
Reproachful expressions or remarks show that you are disappointed, upset, or angry because someone has done something wrong.

grab ^{복습}
[græb]

v. 부여잡다, 움켜쥐다; n. 부여잡기
If you grab something, you take it or pick it up suddenly and roughly.

rifle[raifl]
① n. 라이플총 ② vt. 샅샅이 뒤지다; 강탈하다
A rifle is a gun with a long barrel.

will[wil]
v. 의지를 발동하다; 바라다, 원하다; 뜻하다; n. 의지; 유언장
If you will something to happen, you try to make it happen by using mental effort rather than physical effort.

damp[dæmp]
a. 축축한; n. 습기
Something that is damp is slightly wet.

pole[poul]
n. 막대, 기둥; 장대; 극
A pole is a long thin piece of wood or metal, used especially for supporting things.

concentrate[kánsəntrèit]
v. 집중하다, 전념하다
If you concentrate on something, you give all your attention to it.

recall[rikɔ́:l]
vt. 생각해 내다, 상기하다, 소환하다; n. 회상, 상기
When you recall something, you remember it and tell others about it.

lie[lai]
vi. 눕다, 누워 있다; 놓여 있다, 위치하다
If you are lying somewhere, you are in a horizontal position and are not standing or sitting.

blanket[blǽŋkit]
n. 담요, 덮개; vt. 담요로 덮다[싸다]
A blanket is a large square or rectangular piece of thick cloth, especially one which you put on a bed to keep you warm.

snore[snɔ:r]
v. 코를 골다
When someone who is asleep snores, they make a loud noise each time they breathe.

squeeze[skwi:z]
vt. 꽉 쥐다[죄다], 압착하다; n. 압착, 짜냄; 꽉 끌어안음
If you squeeze something, you press it firmly, usually with your hands.

first-ever[fə:rst-évər]
a. 생전 처음의, 사상 최초의
Something that is the first-ever one of its kind has never happened before.

seep[si:p]
vi. 스며 나오다, 새다
If something such as liquid or gas seeps somewhere, it flows slowly and in small amounts into a place where it should not go.

suitcase[súːtkèis]
n. 여행 가방
A suitcase is a box or bag with a handle and a hard frame in which you carry your clothes when you are traveling.

carve[ka:rv]
vt. 새기다, 조각하다
If you carve an object, you make it by cutting it out of a substance such as wood or stone.

beak[bi:k]
n. 새의 부리
A bird's beak is the hard curved or pointed part of its mouth.

break into
phrasal v. 갑자기 ~하기 시작하다
To break into something means to begin doing it suddenly.

94

recliner^{복습}
[rikláinər]

n. (= recliner chair) 안락의자, 기대는 것
A recliner is a type of armchair having a back that can be adjusted to slope at various angles.

bald^{복습}
[bɔːld]

a. (머리 등이) 벗어진, 대머리의; vi. 머리가 벗어지다
Someone who is bald has little or no hair on the top of their head.

spot^{복습}
[spat]

n. 장소, 지점; 반점, 얼룩; vt. 발견하다, 분별하다
You can refer to a particular place as a spot.

make sense^{복습}

idiom 이해하다, 뜻을 알다; 뜻이 통하다, 도리에 맞다
If you make sense of something that is difficult or not very clear, you understand it.

compare**
[kəmpéər]

v. 비교하다, 대조하다; 비유하다
When you compare things, you consider them and discover the differences or similarities between them.

jerk^{복습}
[dʒəːrk]

① v. 갑자기 움직이다; n. 갑자기 움직임; 반사 운동; ② n. 바보, 멍청이
If you jerk something or someone in a particular direction, or they jerk in a particular direction, they move a short distance very suddenly and quickly.

sigh^{복습}
[sai]

v. 한숨 쉬다; n. 한숨, 탄식
When you sigh, you let out a deep breath, as a way of expressing feelings such as disappointment, tiredness, or pleasure.

creak*
[kriːk]

v. 삐걱거리(게 하)다; n. 삐걱거리는 소리
If something creaks, it makes a short, high-pitched sound when it moves.

apply**
[əplái]

vt. 바르다; 적용하다, 응용하다; 신청하다, 응시하다
If you apply something to a surface, you put it on or rub it into the surface.

ointment^{복습}
[ɔ́intmənt]

n. 연고, 고약(膏藥)
An ointment is a smooth thick substance that is put on sore skin or a wound to help it heal.

1. How did Willie May recognize what Rob gave her?

    A. She needed to look at it carefully.

    B. She needed to smell it.

    C. She only needed to hold it without looking at it.

    D. She needed Rob to describe it to her.

2. How did the carving make Willie May feel?

    A. It made her feel sad over what she had lost.

    B. It made her feel good and soothed her heart.

    C. It made her feel upset to remember painful memories.

    D. It made her feel like owning another bird like Cricket.

3. What did Rob do to help Willie May at the motel?

    A. He helped her strip dirty sheets from beds.

    B. He helped her mop the floors.

    C. He helped her wash dirty walls.

    D. He helped her empty the garbage.

4. What happened to the clothes that Rob had given to Sistine?
   A. Sistine had forgotten them in her locker at school.
   B. Sistine's mother had decided to fix them up for her.
   C. Sistine's mother had put them in the laundry to clean them.
   D. Sistine's mother had taken them away from her.

5. How did Sistine feel about fights at school?
   A. She wanted to avoid fights.
   B. She wanted to get in fights.
   C. She never wanted to hit back.
   D. She liked watching other people fight.

6. How did Rob feel when Sistine saw something beautiful?
   A. He liked it because her voiced changed.
   B. He hated it because her voice changed.
   C. He liked it because the look in her eyes changed.
   D. He hated it because the look in her eyes changed.

Check Your Reading Speed

1분에 몇 단어를 읽는지 리딩 속도를 측정해보세요.

$$\frac{483 \text{ words}}{\text{reading time ( ) sec}} \times 60 = (\quad) \text{ WPM}$$

Build Your Vocabulary

laundry 복습
[lɔ́:ndri]
n. 세탁물; 세탁소 (laundry room n. 세탁실)
Laundry is used to refer to clothes, sheets, and towels that are about to be washed, are being washed, or have just been washed.

foldup
[fóuldʌp]
a. 접을 수 있는
A foldup thing is that you can bend or fold it so that it is smaller.

cigarette 복습
[sigərét]
n. 담배
Cigarettes are small tubes of paper containing tobacco which people smoke.

shifty
[ʃífti]
a. 의문스러운, 둘러대는, 꾀를 부리는
Someone who looks shifty gives the impression of being dishonest.

nerve**
[nə:rv]
n. (어려움에 맞서는) 대담성, 용기; 신경
If you refer to someone's nerves, you mean their ability to cope with problems such as stress, worry, and danger.

enormous 복습
[inɔ́:rməs]
a. 엄청난, 거대한, 막대한
You can use enormous to emphasize the great degree or extent of something.

palm 복습
[pa:m]
① n. 손바닥 ② n. [식물] 종려나무, 야자나무
The palm of your hand is the inside part.

puff*
[pʌf]
v. (연기를) 내뿜다; 숨을 헐떡이다; 부풀어 오르다; n. 훅 불기, 숨, 입김
If someone puffs at a cigarette, cigar, or pipe, they smoke it.

ash*
[æʃ]
n. 재; 유해
Ash is the gray or black powdery substance that is left after something is burned.

tremble 복습
[trembl]
v. 흔들리다; (공포·추위·피로 등으로) 떨(리)다; n. 떨림; 진동
If something trembles, it shakes slightly.

frighten**
[fraitn]
v. 놀라게 하다, 섬뜩하게 하다; 기겁하다
If something or someone frightens you, they cause you to suddenly feel afraid, anxious, or nervous.

soothe*
[su:ð]
v. 달래다, 진정시키다
If you soothe someone who is angry or upset, you make them feel calmer.

strip
[strip]
v. 벗기다, 떼어내다; n. 좁고 긴 땅; 길고 가느다란 조각
To strip something means to remove everything that covers it.

jingle 복습
[ʤíŋgl]

v. 짤랑짤랑 소리를 내다; n. 딸랑딸랑 울리는 소리
When something jingles or when you jingle it, it makes a gentle ringing noise, like small bells.

demand 복습
[dimǽnd]

vt. 묻다, 요구하다, 청구하다; n. 요구, 수요
If you demand something such as information or action, you ask for it in a very forceful way.

Check Your Reading Speed

1분에 몇 단어를 읽는지 리딩 속도를 측정해보세요.

$$\frac{692 \text{ words}}{\text{reading time (\quad) sec}} \times 60 = (\quad) \text{ WPM}$$

Build Your Vocabulary

prophetess ^{복습}
[práfitis]

n. 여자 예언자
A prophetess is a female who is believed to be chosen by God to say the things that God wants to tell people.

skin ^{복습}
[skin]

v. 생채기 내다, 스쳐서 상처를 입히다; 껍질을 벗기다; n. 피부; 가죽
If one's knee or elbow is skinned, it is injured by scraping.

bleed ^{복습}
[bli:d]

v. 피가 나다, 출혈하다
When you bleed, you lose blood from your body as a result of injury or illness.

swollen
[swóulən]

a. 부어오른, 부푼
If a part of your body is swollen, it is larger and rounder than normal, usually as a result of injury or illness.

vacuum[*]
[vǽkjuəm]

v. 진공청소기로 청소하다; n. 진공; 공허, 공백
If you vacuum something, you clean it using a vacuum cleaner.

purposeful
[pə́:rpəsfəl]

a. 목적이 있는, 의도적인 (purposefully ad. 단호하게, 의미심장하게)
If someone is purposeful, they show that they have a definite aim and a strong desire to achieve it.

whirl ^{복습}
[hwə:rl]

v. 빙글 돌다, 선회하다
If something or someone whirls around or if you whirl them around, they move around or turn around very quickly.

face ^{복습}
[feis]

v. ~을 마주보다, 향하다; 직면하다, 직시하다
If someone or something faces a particular thing, person, or direction, they are positioned opposite them or are looking in that direction.

keep up

phrasal v. 뒤떨어지지 않다; 지속하다, 유지하다
If you keep up with someone or something that is moving near you, you move at the same speed.

shag ^{복습}
[ʃæg]

n. 보풀, 뒤얽힌 거친 털(뭉치)
A shag carpet is a fabric with long coarse nap.

tap ^{복습}
[tæp]

① v. 가볍게 두드리다; n. 가볍게 두드리기 ② n. 주둥이, (수도 등의) 꼭지
If you tap something, you hit it with a quick light blow or a series of quick light blows.

fist ^{복습}
[fist]

n. (쥔) 주먹
Your hand is referred to as your fist when you have bent your fingers in toward the palm in order to hit someone.

100

clench
[klentʃ]

v. (손을) 꽉 쥐다; (이를) 악물다; n. 단단히 쥐기; 이를 악물기
When you clench your fist or your fist clenches, you curl your fingers up tightly, usually because you are very angry.

roar^{복습}
[rɔːr]

n. 으르렁거리는 소리; 외치는 소리, 와자지껄함;
vi. (기계 등이) 큰 소리 내며 움직이다; (큰 짐승 등이) 으르렁거리다, 고함치다
If something roars, it makes a very loud noise.

bend^{복습}
[bend]

v. (bent–bent) 구부리다, 굽히다; 구부러지다, 휘다; n. 커브, 굽음
When you bend a part of your body such as your arm or leg, or when it bends, you change its position so that it is no longer straight.

ball***
[bɔːl]

v. (실 등을) 둥글게 뭉치다; 공이 되다; 한 덩어리가 되다; n. 공, 공 모양의 것
When you ball something that is usually flat up or when it balls up, you make it into the shape of a ball.

uncurl
[ʌnkəːrl]

v. 펴다, 펴지다
When you uncurl something, you make it move out of a curled or rolled up position.

utter*
[ʌ́tər]

① v. 발언하다, 입을 열다 ② a. 완전한, 전적인, 절대적인
If someone utters sounds or words, they say them.

punch^{복습}
[pʌntʃ]

v. 세게 치다, 강타하다, 두드리다; (키를) 입력하다; n. 주먹질, 펀치
If you punch someone or something, you hit them hard with your fist.

poem^{복습}
[pouəm]

n. 시, 운문
A poem is a piece of writing in which the words are chosen for their beauty and sound and are carefully arranged, often in short lines which rhyme.

dazzle*
[dǽzl]

v. 눈부시게 하다; n. 눈부심 (dazzling a. 눈부신)
If someone or something dazzles you, you are extremely impressed by their skill, qualities, or beauty.

fair**
[fɛ́ər]

a. 공정한, 공평한; 정당한; 상당한 (unfairly ad. 불공평하게)
Something or someone that is fair is reasonable, right, and just.

dust*
[dʌst]

n. 먼지, 티끌; v. 먼지를 털다[닦다]
Dust is the very small pieces of dirt which you find inside buildings, for example on furniture, floors, or lights.

exclaim*
[ikskléim]

v. 외치다, 소리치다
If you exclaim, you say or shout something suddenly because of surprise, fear and pleasure.

hiss*
[his]

n. 쉿(제지·힐책의 소리); v. 쉿 하는 소리를 내다
If people hiss at someone such as a performer or a person making a speech, they express their disapproval or dislike of that person by making long loud 's' sounds.

disapproval*
[dìsəprúːvəl]

n. 불찬성, 못마땅함, 불만
If you feel or show disapproval of something or someone, you feel or show that you do not approve of them.

1. What was Willie May's opinion on the tiger?
    A. The tiger belonged back in its home country.
    B. The tiger could live with the panthers in the woods.
    C. They could all take care of the tiger together and find it food.
    D. The tiger was better as it was in the cage than in the woods.

2. What did Rob say in response to Sistine telling them her father was coming?
    A. He said that Sistine's father would come after more than a year.
    B. He said that his father would stop Sistine's father from freeing the tiger.
    C. He said Sistine's father was a liar and would not come.
    D. He said that Sistine's father died but she could not handle the truth.

3. What two things did Rob connect with the idea of rising up?
    A. The tiger and his sadness
    B. The tiger and his anger
    C. The tiger and Sistine's anger
    D. Sistine's anger and his sadness

4. Why did Rob run toward Sistine as she walked away from the motel?

   A. He wanted to tell her to never come back to the motel again.

   B. He wanted to tell her to think about why they have to keep the tiger caged.

   C. He wanted to tell her that he planned to let the tiger go.

   D. He wanted her to apologize to him.

5. What truth about Beauchamp and the tiger did Sistine recognize?

   A. Beauchamp loved tigers but was a very busy man.

   B. Beauchamp was afraid of the tiger and made Rob feed it.

   C. Beauchamp had no interest in animals or people.

   D. Beauchamp wanted to sell the tiger to Rob.

6. How did Sistine behave toward Beauchamp that surprised Rob?

   A. She behaved sweetly.

   B. She behaved shyly.

   C. She behaved rudely.

   D. She behaved as if she had met him before.

Check Your Reading Speed

1분에 몇 단어를 읽는지 리딩 속도를 측정해보세요.

$$\frac{674 \text{ words}}{\text{reading time ( ) sec}} \times 60 = (\ ) \text{ WPM}$$

Build Your Vocabulary

chew
[ʧuː]
v. 씹다, 씹어서 으깨다
If you chew gum, you keep biting it and moving it around your mouth to taste the flavor of it.

cigarette
[sigərét]
n. 담배
Cigarettes are small tubes of paper containing tobacco which people smoke.

stare
[stɛər]
v. 응시하다, 뚫어지게 보다
If you stare at someone or something, you look at them for a long time.

pace
[peis]
v. 왔다 갔다 하다, 천천히 걷다; n. 걸음걸이; 속도
If you pace a small area, you keep walking up and down it, because you are anxious or impatient.

doubt
[daut]
v. 의심하다, 의혹을 품다; n. 의심; 회의
If you have doubt or doubts about something, you feel uncertain about it and do not know whether it is true or possible.

fierce
[fiərs]
a. 사나운; 격렬한, 지독한 (fierceness n. 사나움; 격렬함)
A fierce animal or person is very aggressive or angry.

disgust [*]
[disgʌst]
n. 싫음, 혐오감; vt. 역겹게 하다, 넌더리나게 하다
Disgust is a feeling of very strong dislike or disapproval.

demand
[dimǽnd]
vt. 요구하다, 묻다, 청구하다; n. 요구, 수요
If you demand something such as information or action, you ask for it in a very forceful way.

flood ^{**}
[flʌd]
v. 물밀듯이 밀려들다, 쇄도하다; 넘치다, 범람하다; n. 홍수; 다수
If an emotion, feeling, or thought floods you, you suddenly feel it very intensely.

relief
[rilíːf]
n. 안심, 안도
If you feel a sense of relief, you feel happy because something unpleasant has not happened or is no longer happening.

argue
[áːrgjuː]
v. 주장하다, 논쟁하다
If you argue that something is true, you state it and give the reasons why you think it is true.

accuse [*]
[əkjúːz]
v. 비난하다, 고발하다
If you accuse someone of doing something wrong or dishonest, you say or tell them that you believe that they did it.

104

prophetess ^{복습}
[práfitis]

n. 여자 예언자
A prophetess is a female who is believed to be chosen by God to say the things that God wants to tell people.

mutter ^{복습}
[mʌ́tər]

v. 중얼거리다, 불평하다; n. 중얼거림, 불평
If you mutter, you speak very quietly so that you cannot easily be heard, often because you are complaining about something.

count*
[kaunt]

v. 중요하다; 포함시키다; 세다, 계산하다; n. 계산, 셈
If something or someone counts for something or counts, they are important or valuable.

set free ^{복습}

phrasal v. (사람·동물을) 자유롭게 하다, 석방하다
If you set free someone or something, it means you grant freedom to them.

amaze ^{복습}
[əméiz]

vt. 깜짝 놀라게 하다 (amazed a. 놀란)
If something amazes you, it surprises you very much.

glow ^{복습}
[glou]

v. 빛을 내다, 빛나다; n. 빛, 밝음
If something glows, it produces a dull, steady light.

consider*
[kənsídər]

v. 고려하다, 숙고하다
If you consider something, you think about it carefully.

shard
[ʃɑːrd]

n. 파편, (특히 도기의) 사금파리
Shards are pieces of broken glass, pottery, or metal.

shrug ^{복습}
[ʃrʌg]

v. (어깨를) 으쓱하다; n. (양 손바닥을 내보이면서 어깨를) 으쓱하기
If you shrug, you raise your shoulders to show that you are not interested in something or that you do not know or care about something.

scratch ^{복습}
[skrætʃ]

v. 긁다; 할퀴다, 생채기를 내다; n. 긁기; 긁힌 자국, 긁는 소리
If you scratch yourself, you rub your fingernails against your skin because it is itching.

dig ^{복습}
[dig]

v. 파헤치다, 파다; 찌르다; n. 파기
If you dig into something such as a deep container, you put your hand in it to search for something.

itch ^{복습}
[itʃ]

n. 가려움; vi. 가렵다, 근질근질하다
An itch is an uncomfortable feeling on your skin that makes you want to rub it with your nails.

serve ^{복습}
[səːrv]

v. 보복하다, 인과응보다; 식사 시중을 들다, (음식을) 제공하다; 근무하다; (특정한 용도로) 쓰일 수 있다
If you say it serves someone right when something unpleasant happens to them, you mean that it is their own fault and they deserve it.

grab ^{복습}
[græb]

v. 부여잡다, 움켜쥐다; n. 부여잡기
If you grab something, you take it or pick it up suddenly and roughly.

remind ^{복습}
[rimáind]

vt. 생각나게 하다, 상기시키다, 일깨우다
If someone reminds you of a fact or event that you already know about, they say something which makes you think about it.

Check Your Reading Speed

1분에 몇 단어를 읽는지 리딩 속도를 측정해보세요.

$$\frac{596 \text{ words}}{\text{reading time (} \quad \text{) sec}} \times 60 = (\quad) \text{ WPM}$$

Build Your Vocabulary

highway 복습
[háiwèi]

n. 고속도로
A highway is a main road, especially one that connects towns or cities.

miraculous
[mirækjələs]

a. 기적적인, 놀랄 만한 (miraculously ad. 기적적으로, 놀랄 만하게)
If you describe a good event as miraculous, you mean that it is very surprising and unexpected.

glow 복습
[glou]

v. 빛을 내다, 빛나다; n. 빛, 밝음
If something glows, it produces a dull, steady light.

horizon **
[həráizn]

n. 지평선, 수평선
The horizon is the line in the far distance where the sky seems to meet the land or the sea.

catch up 복습

phrasal v. 따라잡다, 따라가다
If you catch up with someone, you reach them by walking faster than them.

squint 복습
[skwint]

v. 실눈으로 보다; 곁눈질을 하다; a. 사시의; 곁눈질하는
If you squint at something, you look at it with your eyes partly closed.

conjure
[kándʒər]

v. ~을 (요술로) 불러내다, 마법을 걸다; 마음속에 그려내다
If you conjure something out of nothing, you make it appear as if by magic.

exist **
[igzíst]

v. 존재하다; 살아가다
If something exists, it is present in the world as a real thing.

whisper 복습
[hwíspər]

v. 속삭이다; n. 속삭임; 속삭이는 소리
When you whisper, you say something very quietly.

nod 복습
[nɔd]

v. 끄덕이다, 끄덕여 표시하다; n. (동의·인사·신호·명령의) 끄덕임
If you nod, you move your head downward and upward to show agreement, understanding, or approval.

pull over

phrasal v. 차를 한쪽에 대다
When you pull over a motor vehicle, you halt it at the side of the road.

holler 복습
[hálər]

v. 고함지르다; 큰 소리로 부르다; n. 외침, 큰 소리
If you holler, you shout loudly.

shrug ^{복습}
[ʃrʌg]

v. (어깨를) 으쓱하다; n. (양 손바닥을 내보이면서 어깨를) 으쓱하기
If you shrug, you raise your shoulders to show that you are not interested in something or that you do not know or care about something.

roar ^{복습}
[rɔːr]

vi. 고함치다; (큰 짐승 등이) 으르렁거리다; (기계 등이) 큰 소리 내며 움직이다; n. 외치는 소리, 왁자지껄함; 으르렁거리는 소리
If someone roars, they shout something in a very loud voice.

pocket^{**}
[pákit]

vt. 호주머니에 넣다; n. 호주머니
If someone pockets something, they put it in their pocket, for example because they want to steal it or hide it.

thump ^{복습}
[θʌmp]

v. 치다, 두드리다; n. 쿵[탁] 하는 소리; (세게) 치기
When your heart thumps, it beats strongly and quickly, usually because you are afraid or excited.

caution^{**}
[kɔ́ːʃən]

v. ~에게 경고하다, 주의시키다; n. 경고, 주의; 조심, 신중
If someone cautions you, they warn you about problems or danger.

beat ^{복습}
[biːt]

v. (심장이) 고동치다; 때리다, 치다, 두드리다; 패배시키다, 이기다; n. [음악] 박자
When your heart or pulse beats, it continually makes regular rhythmic movements.

chase ^{복습}
[ʧeis]

v. 뒤쫓다, 추적하다; 추구하다; n. 추적; 추구
If you chase someone, or chase after them, you run after them or follow them quickly in order to catch or reach them.

pound[*]
[paund]

① v. 마구 치다, 세게 두드리다; 쿵쿵 울리다; n. 타격 ② n. 파운드(무게의 단위) ③ n. 울타리, 우리
If you pound something or pound on it, you hit it with great force, usually loudly and repeatedly.

burst into flame(s)

idiom 갑자기 타오르다, 화가 발끈 일어나다
If something bursts into flames or bursts into flame, it suddenly starts burning strongly.

worth^{**}
[wəːrθ]

a. ~의 가치가 있는; n. 가치, 값어치
If something is worth a particular action, or if an action is worth doing, it is considered to be important enough for that action.

lean ^{복습}
[liːn]

① v. 몸을 구부리다, 기울다; 기대다, 의지하다 ② a. 야윈, 마른
When you lean in a particular direction, you bend your body in that direction.

manly
[mǽnli]

a. 남자다운
If you describe a man's behavior or appearance as manly, you approve of it because it shows qualities that are considered typical of a man, such as strength or courage.

wink ^{복습}
[wiŋk]

v. 윙크[눈짓]하다; 반짝거리다, 깜박이다
When you wink at someone, you look toward them and close one eye very briefly, usually as a signal that something is a joke or a secret.

toothpick ^{복습}
[túːθpìk]

n. 이쑤시개
A toothpick is a small stick which you use to remove food from between your teeth.

wiggle
[wigl]

v. (좌우로) 움직이다; (몸을) 뒤흔들다; n. 뒤흔듦

If you wiggle something or if it wiggles, it moves up and down or from side to side in small quick movements.

squeeze ^{복습}
[skwi:z]

vt. 꽉 쥐다[죄다], 압착하다; n. 압착, 짜냄; 꽉 끌어안음

If you squeeze something, you press it firmly, usually with your hands.

swagger ^{복습}
[swǽgər]

vi. 뽐내며 걷다; 으스대다

If you swagger, you walk in a very proud, confident way, holding your body upright and swinging your hips.

feed ^{복습}
[fi:d]

v. 음식[먹이]을 주다, 먹이다; 공급하다; n. 먹이, 사료

If you feed a person or animal, you give them food to eat and sometimes actually put it in their mouths.

toss ^{복습}
[tɔːs]

v. (머리 등을) 갑자기 쳐들다; 던지다, 내던지다; 뒹굴다, 뒤척이다

If you toss your head or toss your hair, you move your head backward, quickly and suddenly, often as a way of expressing an emotion such as anger or contempt.

matter ^{복습}
[mǽtər]

vi. 중요하다; n. 물질, 문제, 일

If you say that something does matter, you mean that it is important to you because it does have an effect on you or on a particular situation.

set free ^{복습}

phrasal v. (사람·동물을) 자유롭게 하다, 석방하다

If you set free someone or something, it means you grant freedom to them.

108

1. Why was Sistine confident that the tiger would not eat them?
   A. They had just fed him a lot of meat so that his stomach was full now.
   B. The tiger would be too shocked by the door opening to attack them.
   C. The tiger would only see the exit and ignore them completely.
   D. They were his emancipators and he would leave them alone out of gratitude.

2. How did the tiger react when the door opened?
   A. He immediately ran out the door.
   B. He continued pacing back and forth, ignoring the open door.
   C. He stopped pacing and stared at the door for a long time.
   D. He looked at the open door and sat down in his cage.

3. Which of the following is NOT something the tiger did after he left the cage?
   A. He put his nose up and sniffed.
   B. He looked at Rob and Sistine.
   C. He ran through the woods.
   D. He roared at Rob and Sistine.

4. What did Rob tell his father after hitting him was useless?
   A. He needed his mother more than his father.
   B. He needed to move away from Lister.
   C. He needed his father to learn to cook better.
   D. He needed to go see a tiger at the zoo.

5. What did Rob do as his father held him and how did his father react?
   A. Rob cried and his father was angry because he told him not to cry.
   B. Rob cried and his father cried as well and reassured Rob.
   C. Rob pushed him away and his father yelled at him.
   D. Rob tried pushing him away but his father held him silently.

6. Why had Rob's father come with the gun?
   A. He was angry with Beauchamp and was going to threaten him.
   B. He was going to hunt in the wood around the motel.
   C. Willie May had told him to sell the gun in town for money.
   D. Willie May had told him about the tiger and Rob's plan to free him.

7. What did Sistine say they had to do for the tiger?
   A. They had to send it back to its home country.
   B. They had to take him to a vet to cremate him.
   C. They had to hold a funeral for him.
   D. They had to keep it a secret from Beauchamp.

Check Your Reading Speed

1분에 몇 단어를 읽는지 리딩 속도를 측정해보세요.

$$\frac{432 \text{ words}}{\text{reading time ( ) sec}} \times 60 = (\quad) \text{ WPM}$$

Build Your Vocabulary

slide[*]
[slaid]
v. (slid–slid) 미끄러지다. 미끄러지듯 움직이다
When something slides somewhere or when you slide it there, it moves there smoothly over or against something.

smooth[복습]
[smuːð]
a. 매끄러운, 반들반들한; 유창한; v. 매끄럽게 하다[되다] (smoothly ad. 매끄럽게)
A smooth surface has no roughness, lumps, or holes.

dizzy[*]
[dízi]
a. 현기증 나는, 아찔한
If you feel dizzy, you feel as if everything is spinning round and being unable to balance.

amaze[복습]
[əméiz]
vt. 깜짝 놀라게 하다 (amazement n. 놀람, 경탄)
If something amazes you, it surprises you very much.

pound[복습]
[paund]
① v. 마구 치다, 세게 두드리다; 쿵쿵 울리다; n. 타격 ② n. 파운드(무게의 단위) ③ n. 울타리, 우리
If you pound something or pound on it, you hit it with great force, usually loudly and repeatedly.

flutter[*]
[flʌtər]
v. 펄럭이다, 흔들다; (새 등이) 파닥이다, 날갯짓하다; n. 펄럭임
If something thin or light flutters, or if you flutter it, it moves up and down or from side to side with a lot of quick, light movements.

gratitude[**]
[grǽtətjùːd]
n. 감사, 고마움
Gratitude is the state of feeling grateful.

emancipator
[imǽnsəpèitər]
n. 해방자
An emancipator is someone who frees others from bondage.

fling[**]
[fliŋ]
vt. (flung–flung) (문 등을) 왈칵 열다; 내던지다, 던지다
If you fling something into a particular place or position, you put it there in a quick or angry way.

ignore[복습]
[ignɔ́ːr]
vt. 무시하다, 모르는 체하다
If you ignore someone or something, you pay no attention to them.

pace[복습]
[peis]
v. 왔다 갔다 하다, 천천히 걷다; n. 걸음걸이; 속도
If you pace a small area, you keep walking up and down it, because you are anxious or impatient.

oblivious
[əblíviəs]
a. 의식하지 못하는, 안중에 없는
If you are oblivious to something or oblivious of it, you are not aware of it.

creep^{복습}
[kri:p]

vi. (crept–crept) 살금살금 걷다, 기다; n. 포복
If something creeps somewhere, it moves very slowly.

grab^{복습}
[græb]

v. 부여잡다, 움켜쥐다; n. 부여잡기
If you grab something, you take it or pick it up suddenly and roughly.

cling*
[kliŋ]

vi. 매달리다, 달라붙다
If you cling to someone or something, you hold onto them tightly.

furious*
[fjúəriəs]

a. 격노한, 몹시 화가 난; 맹렬한
Someone who is furious is extremely angry.

yell^{복습}
[jel]

v. 소리치다, 고함치다; n. 고함소리, 부르짖음
If you yell, you shout loudly, usually because you are excited, angry, or in pain.

howl*
[haul]

v. 짖다, 울부짖다; n. 울부짖는 소리
If a person howls, they make a long, loud cry expressing pain, anger, or unhappiness.

grace*
[greis]

n. 우아, 품위 있음; 은혜, 은총; vt. 우아하게 하다
If someone moves with grace, they move in a smooth, controlled, and attractive way.

delicacy
[délikəsi]

n. 우아함; 섬세함, 예민함
Delicacy is the quality of being easy to break or harm, and refers especially to people or things that are attractive or graceful.

sniff*
[snif]

v. 코를 킁킁거리다, 냄새를 맡다; 콧방귀를 뀌다; n. 냄새 맡음; 콧방귀
When you sniff, you breathe in air through your nose hard enough to make a sound, for example when you are trying not to cry, or in order to show disapproval.

still^{복습}
[stil]

a. 정지한, 움직이지 않는; 조용한, 고요한; ad. 여전히, 아직도
If you stay still, you stay in the same position and do not move.

clap*
[klæp]

v. 박수를 치다
When you clap, you hit your hands together to show appreciation or attract attention.

blaze*
[bleiz]

vi. 타오르다; n. 불꽃, 화염, 섬광
If something blazes with light or color, it is extremely bright.

contain**
[kəntéin]

vt. 포함하다, 담고 있다; 억누르다, 참다
If something such as a box, bag, room, or place contains things, those things are inside it.

leap^{복습}
[li:p]

v. 껑충 뛰다; 뛰어넘다; n. 뜀, 도약
If you leap, you jump high in the air or jump a long distance.

farther^{복습}
[fá:rðər]

ad. (far–farther–farthest) 더 멀리, 더 나아가서
Farther means a greater distance than before or than something else.

set***
[set]

v. (해·달이) 지다; (물건을) 놓다; a. 고정된; n. 한 벌
When the sun sets, it goes below the horizon.

in time^{복습}

idiom 제시간에, 늦지 않고, 때맞추어
If you do something in time, it means that you are not late to do it.

Check Your Reading Speed

1분에 몇 단어를 읽는지 리딩 속도를 측정해보세요.

$$\frac{922 \text{ words}}{\text{reading time ( ) sec}} \times 60 = (\qquad) \text{ WPM}$$

Build Your Vocabulary

flash**
[flæʃ]

n. 번쩍임, 번쩍하는 빛; 순간; v. 번쩍 비추다; 휙 지나가다
A flash is a sudden burst of light or of something shiny or bright.

float^{복습}
[flout]

v. 떠다니다; 뜨다; 띄우다; n. 뜨는 물건, 부유물
Something that floats in or through the air hangs in it or moves slowly and gently through it.

confuse**
[kənfjúːz]

v. 어리둥절하게 하다, 혼동하다 (confused a. 당황한, 어리둥절한)
To confuse someone means to make it difficult for them to know exactly what is happening or what to do.

crack^{복습}
[kræk]

n. 날카로운 소리; 갈라진 금; v. 날카로운 소리가 나게 하다; 금이 가다, 깨다
A crack is a sharp sound, like the sound of a piece of wood breaking.

still^{복습}
[stil]

a. 정지한, 움직이지 않는; 조용한, 고요한; ad. 여전히, 아직도
If you stay still, you stay in the same position and do not move.

stun*
[stʌn]

vt. 어리벙벙하게 하다; 기절시키다; n. 놀라게 함 (stunned a. 어리벙벙한)
If you are stunned by something, you are extremely shocked or surprised by it and are therefore unable to speak or do anything.

whole***
[houl]

a. (사람이) 상처가 없는, 손상되지 않은; 건전[건강]한; 전부의, 모든
If something is whole, it is in one piece and is not broken or damaged.

rifle^{복습}
[raifl]

① n. 라이플총 ② vt. 샅샅이 뒤지다; 강탈하다
A rifle is a gun with a long barrel.

beat^{복습}
[biːt]

v. 때리다, 치다, 두드리다; (심장이) 고동치다; 패배시키다, 이기다; n. [음악] 박자
To beat on, at, or against something means to hit it hard, usually several times or continuously for a period of time.

fist^{복습}
[fist]

n. (쥔) 주먹
Your hand is referred to as your fist when you have bent your fingers in toward the palm in order to hit someone.

blink^{복습}
[bliŋk]

v. 눈을 깜박거리다; (등불·별 등이) 깜박이다; n. 깜박거림
When you blink or when you blink your eyes, you shut your eyes and very quickly open them again.

suitcase^{복습}
[súːtkèis]

n. 여행 가방
A suitcase is a box or bag with a handle and a hard frame in which you carry your clothes when you are traveling.

spring* \
[spriŋ]

v. (sprang–sprung) 튀다, 뛰어오르다; n. 샘, 수원지; (계절) 봄 \
If something springs in a particular direction, it moves suddenly and quickly.

coil* \
[kɔil]

v. (고리 모양으로) 감다, 휘감다; n. (여러 겹으로 둥글게 감아 놓은) 고리 \
If you coil something, you wind it into a series of loops or into the shape of a ring.

explosive* \
[iksplóusiv]

a. 폭발하는, 폭발적인; n. 폭발물, 폭약 \
Something that is explosive is capable of causing an explosion.

whisper^{복습} \
[hwíspəːr]

v. 속삭이다; n. 속삭임; 속삭이는 소리 \
When you whisper, you say something very quietly.

lurch^{복습} \
[ləːrtʃ]

v. 휘청하다, 요동치다, 비틀거리다 \
To lurch means to make a sudden movement, especially forward, in an uncontrolled way.

motion* \
[móuʃən]

n. 움직임, 운동; 동작, 몸짓; v. 몸짓[손짓]으로 신호하다, 지시하다 \
Motion is the activity or process of continually changing position or moving from one place to another.

spin^{복습} \
[spin]

v. 돌(리)다, 맴돌리다; 오래[질질] 끌다; n. 회전 \
If something spins or if you spin it, it turns quickly around a central point.

bury^{복습} \
[béri]

vt. 묻다, 파묻다, 매장하다 \
If you bury your head or face in something, you press your head or face against it, often because you are unhappy.

sweat^{복습} \
[swet]

n. 땀; v. 땀 흘리다; 습기가 차다 \
Sweat is the salty colorless liquid which comes through your skin when you are hot, ill, or afraid.

leak* \
[liːk]

v. 새다, 새게 하다; n. (물·공기·빛 등이) 새는 구멍[곳] \
If a container, pipe, or roof leaks, or if it leaks gas or liquid, there is a small hole or crack in it that lets gas or liquid flow through.

rush** \
[rʌʃ]

n. 돌진, 맹렬하게 흐르기[달리기]; 바쁨; v. 급히 움직이다, 서두르다, 돌진하다 \
A rush is a situation in which you need to go somewhere or do something very quickly.

rock^{복습} \
[rak]

① v. 앞뒤[좌우]로 흔들(리)다, 진동하다; 동요하다 ② n. 바위, 암석 \
When something rocks or when you rock it, it moves slowly and regularly backward and forward or from side to side.

pound^{복습} \
[paund]

① v. 마구 치다, 세게 두드리다; 쿵쿵 울리다; n. 타격 ② n. 파운드(무게의 단위) ③ n. 울타리, 우리 \
If you pound something or pound on it, you hit it with great force, usually loudly and repeatedly.

slide^{복습} \
[slaid]

v. (slid–slid) 미끄러지다, 미끄러지듯 움직이다 \
If you slide somewhere, you move there smoothly and quietly.

sway^{복습} \
[swei]

v. 흔들(리)다, 동요하다; 설득하다; n. 동요 \
When people or things sway, they lean or swing slowly from one side to the other.

figure out

phrasal v. ~을 생각해내다, 발견하다
If you figure out a solution to a problem or the reason for something, you succeed in solving it or understanding it.

bullet^{복습}
[búlit]

n. (소총·권총의) 총탄, 탄환
A bullet is a small piece of metal with a pointed or rounded end, which is fired out of a gun.

twist**
[twist]

v. 비틀다, 돌리다, 꼬다; n. 뒤틀림, 엉킴; 변화
If you twist something, you turn it to make a spiral shape, for example by turning the two ends of it in opposite directions.

wrinkle*
[riŋkl]

v. 주름이 지다, 구겨지다; n. 주름, 잔주름
If cloth wrinkles, or if someone or something wrinkles it, it gets folds or lines in it.

kneel*
[niːl]

vi. (knelt-knelt) 무릎 꿇다
When you kneel, you bend your legs so that your knees are touching the ground.

crouch*
[krautʃ]

v. 몸을 쭈그리다, 쪼그리고 앉다; 웅크리다; n. 웅크림
If you are crouching, your legs are bent under you so that you are close to the ground and leaning forward slightly.

funeral^{복습}
[fjúːnərəl]

n. 장례식
A funeral is the ceremony that is held when the body of someone who has died is buried or cremated.

fallen
[fɔ́ːlən]

a. (사람이) 죽은, 전사한; 누워 있는; 떨어진; v. FALL의 과거분사형
The fallen are soldiers who have died in battle.

warrior*
[wɔ́riəːr]

n. 전사, 무인
A warrior is a fighter or soldier, especially one in former times who was very brave and experienced in fighting.

fur*
[fəːr]

n. 털; 모피
Fur is the thick and usually soft hair that grows on the bodies of many mammals.

116

Chapters Twenty-nine & Thirty

1. What did Sistine do as they buried the tiger?
   A. She sang a song about a tiger that she remembered from her childhood.
   B. She said part of the poem about the tiger burning bright.
   C. She freely expressed how much she loved the tiger.
   D. She put a flower on the tiger's body.

2. What did Willie May do before they covered the tiger's body?
   A. She placed the carving of Cricket on the tiger's body.
   B. She said a prayer for the tiger's spirit.
   C. She moved the tiger's body in a peaceful position.
   D. She buried her pack of cigarettes and gum with the tiger's body.

3. What happened as they filled the grave?
   A. The rain fell down harder.
   B. It became cloudier.
   C. It became sunnier.
   D. It stopped raining but stayed cloudy.

118

4. What did Rob's father do as he applied medicine to Rob's rash?
   A. He talked with Rob about moving on in life.
   B. He whistled a tune about getting better.
   C. He turned on the radio to listen to music.
   D. He sang a song that he had used to sing with Rob's mother.

5. What did Rob and his father decide to tell Beauchamp about the tiger?
   A. They decided to tell him that the tiger broke the cage and his father saved him.
   B. They decided to tell him that his father let the tiger free and Rob shot it.
   C. They decided to tell him that Rob let the tiger free and his father shot it.
   D. They decided to tell him that Willie May let the tiger free and Sistine shot it.

6. Why did Rob not mind the thought of going back to school?
   A. He was more popular after others heard about his tiger.
   B. He could see Sistine at school.
   C. He could defend himself from bullies now.
   D. He could draw pictures freely in school.

7. What did Rob think about doing for Sistine after he woke up from his dream?
   A. He thought about visiting Sistine's house and becoming closer friends.
   B. He thought about giving Sistine some of his best clothes to wear.
   C. He thought about drawing a picture of Sistine riding the tiger through the woods.
   D. He thought about carving a tiger out of wood for Sistine.

Check Your Reading Speed

1분에 몇 단어를 읽는지 리딩 속도를 측정해보세요.

$$\frac{523 \text{ words}}{\text{reading time ( ) sec}} \times 60 = (\qquad) \text{ WPM}$$

Build Your Vocabulary

shovel*
[ʃʌvəl]

n. 삽; v. ~을 삽으로 뜨다[파다], 삽으로 일하다
A shovel is a tool with a long handle that is used for lifting and moving earth, coal, or snow.

dig복습
[dig]

v. 파다, 파헤치다; 찌르다; n. 파기
If people or animals dig, they make a hole in the ground or in a pile of earth, stones, or rubbish.

poem복습
[pouəm]

n. 시, 운문
A poem is a piece of writing in which the words are chosen for their beauty and sound and are carefully arranged, often in short lines which rhyme.

recite*
[risáit]

vt. 읊다, 낭독[암송]하다
When someone recites a poem or other piece of writing, they say it aloud after they have learned it.

immortal*
[imɔ́ːrtl]

a. 불멸의, 죽지 않는; n. 죽지 않는 사람
Someone or something that is immortal is famous and likely to be remembered for a long time.

frame복습
[freim]

vt. 테에 끼우다, ~의 뼈대를 만들다, 짜 맞추다; n. 구조, 골격, 틀
When a picture or photograph is framed, it is put in a frame.

fearful*
[fíərfəl]

a. 무서운, 소름끼치는; 두려워하는, 겁내는
You use fearful to emphasize how serious or bad a situation is.

symmetry
[símətri]

n. (좌우의) 대칭, 균형
Something that has symmetry is symmetrical in shape, design, or structure.

distant**
[dístənt]

a. 먼, 떨어진
Distant means very far away.

dare*
[dɛər]

v. 감히 ~하다, 무릅쓰다, 도전하다
If you dare to do something, you do something which requires a lot of courage.

aspire
[əspáiər]

vi. 열망하다, 갈망하다
If you aspire to something such as an important job, you have a strong desire to achieve it.

bend복습
[bend]

v. (bent-bent) 구부리다, 굽히다; 구부러지다, 휘다; n. 커브, 굽음
When you bend a part of your body such as your arm or leg, or when it bends, you change its position so that it is no longer straight.

lay^{***}
[lei]

v. (laid–laid) 놓다, 눕히다; 알을 낳다
If you lay something somewhere, you put it there in a careful, gentle, or neat way.

company^{***}
[kámpəni]

n. 함께 있음, 교제; 동료, 일행; 회사; v. 따르다, 동행하다
If you keep someone company, you spend time with them and stop them feeling lonely or bored.

grave^{**}
[greiv]

① n. 무덤, 묘 ② a. 중대한, 근엄한
A grave is a place where a dead person is buried.

throat^{복습}
[θrout]

n. 목(구멍) (clear one's throat idiom 목을 가다듬다)
Your throat is the back of your mouth and the top part of the tubes that go down into your stomach and your lungs.

hum^{**}
[hʌm]

v. 웅얼거리다; 콧노래를 부르다; (벌·기계 등이) 윙윙거리다; n. 윙윙(소리)
If something hums, it makes a low continuous noise.

lean^{복습}
[liːn]

① v. 몸을 구부리다, 기울다; 기대다, 의지하다 ② a. 야윈, 마른
When you lean in a particular direction, you bend your body in that direction.

flicker
[flíkər]

v. (등불·희망·빛 등이) 깜박이다; n. 깜박임
If a light or flame flickers, it shines unsteadily.

stare^{복습}
[stɛər]

v. 응시하다, 뚫어지게 보다
If you stare at someone or something, you look at them for a long time.

recognize^{복습}
[rékəgnaiz]

vt. 인지하다, 알아보다
If you recognize someone or something, you know who that person is or what that thing is.

in time^{복습}

idiom 제시간에, 늦지 않고, 때맞추어
If you do something in time, it means that you are not late to do it.

funeral^{복습}
[fjúːnərəl]

n. 장례식
A funeral is the ceremony that is held when the body of someone who has died is buried or cremated.

headstone
[hédstòun]

n. 묘비; 주춧돌
A headstone is a large stone which stands at one end of a grave, usually with the name of the dead person carved on it.

slip^{복습}
[slip]

v. 슬며시 두다; 재빨리 입다; 미끄러지다
If you slip something somewhere, you put it there quickly in a way that does not attract attention.

marvel[*]
[máːrvəl]

v. 놀라다; 이상하게 여기다; n. 놀라운 일, 경이
If you marvel at something, you express your great surprise, wonder, or admiration.

comfort^{복습}
[kʌ́mfərt]

n. 마음이 편안함, 안락; 위로, 위안; vt. 위로[위안]하다, 안심시키다
If you are doing something in comfort, you are physically relaxed and contented, and are not feeling any pain or other unpleasant sensations.

bother ^{복습}
[báðər]

v. 귀찮게 하다. 괴롭히다. 폐 끼치다; 일부러 ～하다. 애를 쓰다

If something bothers you, or if you bother about it, it worries, annoys, or upsets you.

Check Your Reading Speed

1분에 몇 단어를 읽는지 리딩 속도를 측정해보세요.

$$\frac{660 \text{ words}}{\text{reading time ( ) sec}} \times 60 = (\quad) \text{ WPM}$$

Build Your Vocabulary

mine ^{복습}
[main]

v. 채굴하다; n. 광산; 지뢰
When a mineral such as coal, diamonds, or gold is mined, it is obtained from the ground by digging deep holes and tunnels.

throat ^{복습}
[θrout]

n. 목(구멍) (clear one's throat idiom 목을 가다듬다)
Your throat is the back of your mouth and the top part of the tubes that go down into your stomach and your lungs.

coward*
[kauərd]

n. 겁쟁이, 비겁한 사람; a. 겁이 많은, 소심한; 비겁한
If you call someone a coward, you disapprove of them because they are easily frightened and avoid dangerous or difficult situations.

offer ^{복습}
[ɔ́:fər]

v. 제의[제안]하다; 제공하다; n. 제공
If you offer something to someone, you ask them if they would like to have it or use it.

reasonable
[rí:zənəbl]

a. 합당한, 이치에 맞는, 분별 있는
If you say that a decision or action is reasonable, you mean that it is fair and sensible.

predict*
[pridíkt]

v. 예상하다, 예언하다
If you predict an event, you say that it will happen.

nod ^{복습}
[nɔd]

v. 끄덕이다, 끄덕여 표시하다; n. (동의·인사·신호·명령의) 끄덕임
If you nod, you move your head downward and upward to show agreement, understanding, or approval.

aim ^{복습}
[eim]

v. ~할 작정이다; 겨냥을 하다, 목표삼다; n. 겨냥, 조준; 목적, 뜻
If you aim to do something, you decide or want to do it.

principal ^{복습}
[prínsəpəl]

n. 장(長), 교장; a. 주요한, 제1의
The principal of a school is the person in charge of the school.

mess around

idiom 빈둥대다
If you mess around with something, you behave in a silly way with doing it, especially when you should be working or doing something else.

mind ^{복습}
[maind]

v. 싫어하다, 꺼리다; n. 마음, 정신
If you do not mind something, you are not annoyed or bothered by it.

bend ^{복습}
[bend]

v. (bent–bent) 구부리다, 굽히다; 구부러지다, 휘다; n. 커브, 굽음
When you bend a part of your body such as your arm or leg, or when it bends, you change its position so that it is no longer straight.

concentrate^{복습}
[kánsəntrèit]

v. 집중하다, 전념하다
If you concentrate on something, you give all your attention to it.

on account of^{복습}

idiom ~때문에, ~이므로
You use on account of to introduce the reason or explanation for something.

complicate[*]
[kámpləkèit]

vt. 복잡하게 하다, 뒤얽히게 만들다 (complicated a. 복잡한, 뒤얽힌)
To complicate something means to make it more difficult to understand or deal with.

grave^{복습}
[greiv]

① n. 무덤, 묘 ② a. 중대한, 근엄한
A grave is a place where a dead person is buried.

flutter^{복습}
[flʌ́tə:r]

n. 펄럭임; v. (새 등이) 파닥이다, 날갯짓하다; 펄럭이다, 흔들다
If something light such as a small bird or a piece of paper flutters somewhere, it moves through the air with small quick movements.

chase^{복습}
[tʃeis]

v. 뒤쫓다, 추적하다; 추구하다; n. 추적; 추구
If you chase someone, or chase after them, you run after them or follow them quickly in order to catch or reach them.

bump^{복습}
[bʌmp]

v. (쾅 하고) 부딪치다, 충돌하다; n. 충돌; 혹
If you bump into something or someone, you accidentally hit them while you are moving.

ceiling^{복습}
[síːliŋ]

n. 천장
A ceiling is the horizontal surface that forms the top part or roof inside a room.

stare^{복습}
[stɛər]

v. 응시하다, 뚫어지게 보다
If you stare at someone or something, you look at them for a long time.

admire^{**}
[ædmáiər]

v. 감탄하며 바라보다; 존경하다, 칭찬하다
If you admire someone or something, you like and respect them very much.

figure^{복습}
[fígjər]

n. 형태, 형상; 수치, 숫자; 작은 조각상; v. 생각하다, 판단하다, 계산하다
You refer to someone that you can see as a figure when you cannot see them clearly or when you are describing them.

firework^{복습}
[fáiərwɔ́ːrk]

n. 폭죽, 불꽃놀이
Firework is a small device containing powder that burns or explodes and produces bright colored lights and loud noises, used especially at celebrations.

lie^{복습}
[lai]

vi. (lay–lain) 눕다, 누워 있다; 놓여 있다, 위치하다
If you are lying somewhere, you are in a horizontal position and are not standing or sitting.

poke[*]
[pouk]

v. 들이대다, 쑥 내밀다; 찌르다, 쑤시다; n. 찌름, 쑤심
If something pokes out of or through another thing, you can see part of it appearing from behind or underneath the other thing.

consider^{복습}
[kənsídər]

v. 고려하다, 숙고하다
If you consider something, you think about it carefully.

compete**
[kəmpíːt]

vi. 겨루다, 경쟁하다
If you compete with someone for something, you try to get it for yourself and stop the other person getting it.

수고하셨습니다!

드디어 끝까지 다 읽으셨군요! 축하드립니다! 여러분은 이 책을 통해 총 33,585개의 단어를 읽으셨고, 1,026개 이상의 어휘와 표현들을 익히셨습니다. 이 책에 나온 어휘는 다른 원서를 읽을 때에도 빈번히 만날 수 있는 필수 어휘들입니다. 이 책을 읽었던 경험은 비슷한 수준의 다른 원서들을 읽을 때 큰 도움이 될 것입니다.

이제 자신의 상황에 맞게 원서를 반복해서 읽거나, 오디오북을 들어 볼 수 있습니다. 혹은 비슷한 수준의 다른 원서를 찾아 읽는 것도 좋습니다. 일단 원서를 완독한 뒤에 어떻게 계속 영어 공부를 이어갈 수 있을지, 도움말을 꼼꼼히 살펴보고 각자 상황에 맞게 적용해 보세요!

리딩(Reading)을 확실하게 다지고 싶다면? 반복해서 읽어 보세요!

리딩 실력을 탄탄하게 다지고 싶다면, 같은 원서를 2-3번 반복해서 읽을 것을 권합니다. 같은 책을 여러 번 읽으면 지루할 것 같지만, 꼭 그렇지도 않습니다. 반복해서 읽을 때 처음과 주안점을 다르게 두면, 전혀 다른 느낌으로 재미있게 읽을 수 있습니다.

처음 원서를 읽을 때는 생소한 단어들과 스토리로 인해 읽으면서 곧바로 이해하기가 매우 힘들 수 있습니다. 전체 맥락을 잡고 읽어도 약간 버거운 느낌이지요. 하지만 반복해서 읽기 시작하면 달라집니다. 일단 내용을 파악한 상황이기 때문에 문장 구조나 어휘의 활용에 더 집중하게 되고, 조금 더 깊이 있게 읽을 수 있습니다. 좋은 표현과 문장을 수집하고 메모할 만한 여유도 생기게 되지요. 어휘도 많이 익숙해졌기 때문에 리딩 속도에도 탄력이 붙습니다. 처음 읽을 때는 '내용'에서 재미를 느꼈다면, 반복해서 읽을 때에는 '영어'에서 재미를 느끼게 되는 것입니다. 따라서 리딩 실력을 더욱 확고하게 다지고자 한다면, 같은 책을 2-3회 정도 반복해서 읽을 것을 권해 드립니다.

리스닝(Listening) 실력을 늘리고 싶다면?
귀를 통해서 읽어 보세요!

많은 영어 학습자들이 '리스닝이 안 돼서 문제'라고 한탄합니다. 그리고 리스닝 실력을 늘리는 방법으로 무슨 뜻인지 몰라도 반복해서 듣는 '무작정 듣기'를 선택합니다. 하지만 뜻도 모르면서 무작정 듣는 일에는 엄청난 인내력이 필요합니다. 그래서 대부분 며칠 시도하다가 포기해 버리고 말지요.

따라서 모르는 내용을 무작정 듣는 것보다는 어느 정도 알고 있는 내용을 반복해서 듣는 것이 더 효과적인 듣기 방법입니다. 그리고 이런 방식의 듣기에 활용할 수 있는 가장 좋은 교재가 오디오북입니다.

리스닝 실력을 향상하고 싶다면, 이 책에서 제공하는 오디오북을 이용해서 듣는 연습을 해 보세요. 활용법은 간단합니다. 일단 책을 한 번 완독했다면, 오디오북을 통해 다시 들어 보는 것입니다. 휴대 기기에 넣어 시간이 날 때 틈틈이 듣는 것도 좋고, 책상에 앉아 눈으로는 텍스트를 보며 귀로 읽는 것도 좋습니다. 이미 읽었던 내용이라 이해하기가 훨씬 수월하고, 애매했던 발음들도 자연스럽게 교정할 수 있습니다. 또 성우의 목소리 연기를 듣다 보면 내용이 더욱 생동감 있게 다가와 이해도가 높아지는 효과도 거둘 수 있습니다.

반대로 듣기에 자신 있는 사람이라면, 책을 읽기 전에 처음부터 오디오북을 먼저 듣는 것도 좋은 방법입니다. 귀를 통해 책을 쭉 읽어 보고, 이후에 다시 눈으로 책을 읽으면서 잘 들리지 않았던 부분을 보충하는 것이지요.

중요한 것은 내용을 따라가면서, 내용에 푹 빠져서 반복해 들어야 한다는 것입니다. 이렇게 연습을 반복해서 눈으로 읽지 않은 책이라도 '귀를 통해' 읽을 수 있을 정도가 되면, 리스닝으로 고생하는 일은 거의 없을 것입니다.

왼쪽의 QR 코드를 스마트폰으로 인식하여 정식 오디오북을 들어 보세요!
더불어 롱테일북스 홈페이지(www.longtailbooks.co.kr)에서도
오디오북 MP3 파일을 다운로드 받을 수 있습니다.

스피킹(Speaking)이 고민이라면? 소리 내어 읽어 보세요!

스피킹 역시 많은 학습자들이 고민하는 부분입니다. 스피킹이 고민이라면, 원서를 큰 소리로 읽는 낭독 훈련(voice reading)을 해 보세요!

'소리 내어 읽는 것이 말하기에 정말로 도움이 될까?'라고 의아한 생각이 들 수도 있습니다. 하지만 인간의 두뇌 입장에서 봤을 때, 성대 구조를 활용해서 '발화'한다는 점에서는 소리 내어 읽기와 말하기에 큰 차이가 없다고 합니다. 소리 내어 읽는 것은 '타인의 생각'을 전달하고, 직접 말하는 것은 '자신의 생각'을 전달한다는 차이가 있을 뿐, 머릿속에서 문장을 처리하고 조음기관(혀와 성대 등)을 움직여 의미를 만든다는 점에서 같은 과정인 것이지요. 따라서 소리 내어 읽는 연습을 꾸준히 하는 것은 스피킹 연습에 큰 도움이 됩니다.

소리 내어 읽기를 하는 방법은 간단합니다. 일단 오디오북을 들으면서 성우의 목소리를 최대한 따라 하며 같이 읽어 보세요. 발음뿐 아니라 억양, 어조, 느낌까지 완벽히 따라 한다고 생각하면서 소리 내어 읽습니다. 따라 읽는 것이 조금 익숙해지면, 옆의 누군가에게 이 책을 읽어 준다는 생각으로 소리 내어 계속 읽어나갑니다. 한 번 눈과 귀로 읽었던 책이기 때문에 보다 수월하게 진행할 수 있고, 자연스럽게 어휘와 표현을 복습하는 효과도 거두게 됩니다. 또 이렇게 소리 내어 읽은 것을 녹음해서 들어 보면 스스로에게도 좋은 피드백이 됩니다.

최근 말하기가 강조되면서 소리 내어 읽기가 크게 각광을 받고 있기는 하지만, 그렇다고 소리 내어 읽기가 무조건 좋은 것만은 아닙니다. 책을 소리 내어 읽다 보면, 무의식적으로 속으로 발음을 하는 습관을 가지게 되어 리딩 속도 자체는 오히려 크게 떨어지는 현상이 발생할 수 있습니다. 따라서 빠른 리딩 속도가 중요한 수험생이나 고학력 학습자들에게는 소리 내어 읽기가 적절하지 않은 방법입니다. 효과가 좋다는 말만 믿고 무턱대고 따라 하기보다는 자신의 필요에 맞게 우선순위를 정하고 원서를 활용하는 것이 좋습니다.

라이팅(Writing)까지 욕심이 난다면? 요약하는 연습을 해 보세요!

원서를 라이팅 연습에 직접적으로 활용하는 데에는 한계가 있지만, 적절히 활용하면 원서도 유용한 라이팅 자료가 될 수 있습니다.

특히 책을 읽고 그 내용을 요약하는 연습은 큰 도움이 됩니다. 요약 훈련의 방식도 간단합니다. 원서를 읽고 그날 읽은 분량만큼 혹은 책을 다 읽고 전체 내용을 기반으로, 책 내용을 한번 요약하고 나의 느낌을 영어로 적어 보는 것입니다.

이때 그 책에 나왔던 단어와 표현을 최대한 활용하여 요약하는 것이 중요합니다. 영어 표현력은 결국 얼마나 다양한 어휘로 많은 표현을 해 보았느냐가 좌우하게 됩니다. 이런 면에서 내가 읽은 책을, 그 책에 나온 문장과 어휘로 다시 표현해 보는 것은 매우 효율적인 방법입니다. 책에 나온 어휘와 표현을 단순히 읽고 무슨 말인지 아는 정도가 아니라, 실제로 직접 활용해서 쓸 수 있을 만큼 확실하게 익히게 되는 것이지요. 여기에 첨삭까지 받을 수 있는 방법이 있다면 금상첨화입니다.

이러한 '표현하기' 연습은 스피킹 훈련에도 그대로 적용될 수 있습니다. 책을 읽고 그 내용을 3분 안에 다른 사람에게 영어로 말하는 연습을 해 보세요. 순발력과 표현력을 기르는 좋은 훈련이 될 것입니다.

꾸준히 원서를 읽고 싶다면? 뉴베리 수상작을 계속 읽어 보세요!

뉴베리 상이 세계 최고 권위의 아동 문학상인 만큼, 그 수상작들은 확실히 완성도를 검증받은 작품이라고 할 수 있습니다. 특히 '쉬운 어휘로 쓰인 깊이 있는 문장'으로 이루어졌다는 점이 영어 학습자들에게 큰 호응을 얻고 있습니다. 이렇게 '검증된 원서'를 꾸준히 읽는 것은 영어 실력 향상에 큰 도움이 됩니다.

아래에 수준별로 제시된 뉴베리 수상작 목록을 보며 적절한 책들을 찾아 계속 읽어 보세요. 꼭 뉴베리 수상작이 아니더라도 마음에 드는 작가의 다른 책을 읽어 보는 것 또한 아주 좋은 방법입니다.

• 영어 초보자도 쉽게 읽을 만한 아주 쉬운 수준. 소리 내어 읽기에도 아주 적합.
Sarah, Plain and Tall*(Medal, 8,331단어), The Hundred Penny Box (Honor, 5,878단어), The Hundred Dresses*(Honor, 7,329단어), My Father's Dragon (Honor, 7,682단어), 26 Fairmount Avenue (Honor, 6,737단어)

• 중·고등학생 정도 영어 학습자라면 쉽게 읽을 수 있는 수준. 소리 내어 읽기에도 비교적 적합한 편.
Because of Winn-Dixie★(Honor, 22,123단어), What Jamie Saw (Honor, 17,203단어), Charlotte's Web (Honor, 31,938단어), Dear Mr. Henshaw (Medal, 18,145단어), Missing May (Medal, 17,509단어)

• 대학생 정도 영어 학습자라면 무난한 수준. 소리 내어 읽기에는 적합하지 않음.
Number The Stars★(Medal, 27,197단어), A Single Shard (Medal, 33,726단어), The Tale of Despereaux★(Medal, 32,375단어), Hatchet★(Medal, 42,328단어), Bridge to Terabithia (Medal, 32,888단어), A Fine White Dust (Honor, 19,022단어), Jennifer, Hecate, Macbeth, William McKinley and Me, Elizabeth (Honor, 23,266단어)

• 원서 완독 경험을 가진 학습자에게 적절한 수준. 소리 내어 읽기에는 적합하지 않음.
The Giver★(Medal, 43,617단어), From the Mixed-Up Files of Mrs. Basil E. Frankweiler (Medal, 30,906단어), The View from Saturday (Medal, 42,685단어), Holes★(Medal, 47,079단어), Criss Cross (Medal, 48,221단어), Walk Two Moons (Medal, 59,400단어), The Graveyard Book (Medal, 67,380단어)

뉴베리 수상작과 뉴베리 수상 작가의 좋은 작품을 엄선한 「뉴베리 컬렉션」에도 위 목록에 있는 도서 중 상당수가 포함될 예정입니다.

★ 「뉴베리 컬렉션」으로 이미 출간된 도서

어떤 책들이 출간되었는지 확인하려면, 지금 인터넷서점에서
뉴베리 컬렉션 을 검색해보세요.

뉴베리 수상작을 동영상 강의로 만나 보세요!

영어원서 전문 동영상 강의 사이트 영서당(yseodang.com)에서는 뉴베리 컬렉션 『Holes』, 『Because of Winn-Dixie』, 『The Miraculous Journey of Edward Tulane』, 『Wayside School 시리즈』 등의 동영상 강의를 제공하고 있습니다. 뉴베리 수상작이라는 최고의 영어 교재와 EBS 출신 인기 강사가 만난 명강의! 지금 사이트를 방문해서 무료 샘플 강의를 들어 보세요!

'스피드 리딩 카페'를 통해 원서 읽기 습관을 길러 보세요!

일상에서 영어를 한마디도 쓰지 않는 비영어권 국가에서 살고 있는 우리가 영어 환경에 가장 쉽고, 편하고, 부담 없이 노출되는 방법은 바로 '영어원서 읽기'입니다. 언제 어디서든 원서를 붙잡고 읽기만 하면 곧바로 영어를 접하는 환경이 만들어지기 때문이지요. 하루에 20분씩만 꾸준히 읽는다면, 1년에 무려 120시간 동안 영어에 노출될 수 있습니다. 이러한 이유 때문에 영어 교육 전문가들이 영어 원서 읽기를 추천하는 것이지요.

하지만 원서 읽기가 좋다는 것을 알아도 막상 꾸준히 읽는 것은 쉽지 않습니다. 그럴 때에는 13만 명 이상의 회원을 보유한 국내 최대 원서 읽기 동호회 〈스피드 리딩 카페〉(cafe.naver. com/readingtc)를 방문해 보세요.

원서별로 정리된 무료 PDF 단어장과 수준별 추천 원서 목록 등 유용한 자료는 물론, 뉴베리 수상작을 포함한 다양한 원서의 리뷰를 무료로 확인할 수 있습니다. 특히 함께 모여서 원서를 읽는 '북클럽'은 중간에 포기하지 않고 원서를 끝까지 읽는 습관을 기르는 데 큰 도움이 될 것입니다.

Answer Key

Chapters One & Two

1. C   Rob liked the sign; he harbored a dim but abiding notion that it would bring him good luck.

2. A   He had been out in the woods behind the Kentucky Star Motel, way out in the woods, not really looking for anything, just wandering, hoping that maybe he would get lost or get eaten by a bear and not have to go to school ever again.

3. B   Rob had a way of not-thinking about things. He imagined himself as a suitcase that was too full, like the one that he had packed when they left Jacksonville after the funeral. He made all his feelings go inside the suitcase; he stuffed them in tight and then sat on the suitcase and locked it shut.

4. B   Billy shoved him hard. And then Norton came swaggering back and leaned over Billy and grabbed hold of Rob's hair with one hand, and with the other hand ground his knuckles into Rob's scalp.

5. C   It hurt, but Rob didn't cry. He never cried. He was a pro at not-crying. He was the best not-crier in the world. It drove Norton and Billy Threemonger wild. And today Rob had the extra power of the tiger. All he had to do was think about it, and he knew there was no way he would cry.

6. D   They were still out in the country, only halfway into town, when the bus lurched to a stop. This was such a surprising development, to have the bus stop halfway through its route, that Norton stopped grinding his knuckles into Rob's scalp and Billy stopped punching Rob in the arm.

Chapters Three & Four

1. D   Nobody wore pink lacy dresses to school. Nobody. Even Rob knew that. He held his breath as he watched the girl walk down the aisle of the bus.

2. B   "Sistine," hooted Billy. "What kind of stupid name is that?" "Like the chapel," she said slowly, making each word clear and strong.

3. D   Rob looked out the window at the gray rain and the gray sky and the grey highway. He thought about the tiger. He thought about God and Adam. And he thought about Sistine. He did not think about the rash. He did not think about his mother. And he did not think about Norton and Billy Threemonger. He kept the suitcase closed.

4. C   "I'm from Philadelphia, Pennsylvania," Sistine said, "home of the Liberty Bell, and I hate the South because the people in it are ignorant. And I'm not staying here in Lister. My father is coming to get me next week."

5. C   He sketched out the tiger, but what he wanted to do was whittle it in wood. His mother had shown him how to whittle, how to take a piece of wood and make it come alive. She taught him when she was sick. He sat on the edge of the bed and watched her tiny white hands closely.

6. A   "Rob," said the teacher, "I need you to go to the principal's office." Rob didn't hear her. He was working on the tiger, trying to remember what his eyes looked like.

7. B   On his way out of the classroom, Jason Uttmeir tripped him and said, "See you later, retard," and Sistine looked up at him with her tiny black eyes. She shot him a look of pure hate.

Chapters Five & Six

1. A   Rob nodded. This was how Mr. Phelmer began all his talks with Rob. He was always worried: worried that Rob did not interact with the other students, worried that he did not communicate, worried that he wasn't doing well, in any way, at school.

2. D   "Here's the situation, Rob. Some of the parents—I won't mention any names—are worried that what you've got there might be contagious, *contagious* meaning something that the other students could possibly catch." Mr. Phelmer cleared his throat again. He stared at Rob.

3. B   "Well," said Mr. Phelmer, "let me tell you what I think. Let me be up-front and honest with you. I think it might be a good idea if we had you stay home for a few days. What we'll do is just give that old medicine more of a chance to kick in, let it start working its magic on you, and then we'll have you come back to school when your legs have cleared up. What do you think about that plan?"

4. C   And then, finally, he smiled. He smiled because he knew something Mr. Phelmer did not know. He knew that his legs would never clear up. He was free.

5. B   He saw her arms still going like mad. "Hey!" he shouted, not meaning to. "Hey!" he shouted again, louder. He moved closer, the drawing of the tiger still in his hand. "Leave her alone!" he shouted, not believing that the words were coming from him.

6. A   They were all looking at him. Waiting. Sistine was waiting, too; waiting for him to do something. He looked down at the ground and saw what they had thrown at her. It was an apple. He stared at it for what seemed like a long time, and when he looked back up, they were all still waiting to see what he would do. And so he ran.

7. B   And he did not know where his drawing of the tiger was, but he still had Mr. Phelmer's note in his back pocket and that was all that truly mattered to him, the note that proved that he would never have to come back.

Chapters Seven & Eight

1. C   "There isn't any place else to sit," she said to him. "This is the last empty seat." Rob shrugged. "It's not like I want to sit here," she said.

2. D   "I know what contagious means," Sistine said. She looked at his legs. And then she did something truly astounding: she closed her eyes and reached out her left hand and placed it on top of Rob's right leg. "Please let me catch it," she whispered.

3. A   Sistine stared at him. "I'll bring you your homework," she said. "I'll bring it to you at the motel."

4. B   His father read the note from the principal slowly, putting his big finger under the words as if they were bugs he was trying to keep still. When he was finally done, he laid the letter on the table and rubbed his eyes with his fingers and sighed. The rain beat a sad rhythm on the roof of the motel. "That stuff ain't nothing anybody else can catch," his father said.

5. A   "Can I go outside?" Rob asked when his father was done. "Naw," his father said. "I don't want that medicine rained off you. It cost too much."

6. C   Rob sat on his bed and started to work on carving the tiger. He had a good piece of maple and his knife was sharp, and in his mind he could see the tiger clearly. But something different came out of the wood. It wasn't a tiger at all. It was a person, with a sharp nose and small eyes and skinny legs. It wasn't until he started working on the dress that Rob realized he was carving Sistine.

7. A   He stayed up late working on the carving, and when he finally fell asleep he dreamed about the tiger, only it wasn't in a cage. It was free and running through the

woods, and there was something on its back, but Rob couldn't tell what it was. As the tiger got closer and closer, Rob saw that the thing was Sistine in her pink party dress. She was riding the tiger. In his dream, Rob waved to her and she waved back at him. But she didn't stop. She and the tiger kept going, past Rob, deeper and deeper into the woods.

Chapters Nine & Ten

1. B   His father woke him up at five-thirty the next morning. "Come on, son," he said, shaking Rob's shoulder. "Come on, you're a working man now. You got to get up." He took his hand away and stood over Rob for a minute more, and then he left.

2. A   In his suitcase of not-thoughts, there were also not-wishes. He kept the lid closed on them, too.

3. D   That was what the sun made him think of. The funeral. And so he didn't care if he ever saw the sun again. He didn't care if the whole state did turn into a swamp.

4. C   "I tell you what," said Willie May. She reached up and adjusted the butterfly clip in her thick black hair. "I'd rather be sweeping up after some pigs in a barn than cleaning up after the people in this place. Pigs at least give you some respect."

5. B   "That's right. Ain't nobody wants this job. I'm the only fool Beauchamp can pay to do it. You got to stay in school," she said, "else you'll end up like me."

6. C   "Sadness," said Willie May, closing her eyes and nodding her head. "You keeping all that sadness down low, in your legs. You not letting it get up to your heart, where it belongs. You got to let that sadness rise on up."

7. D   She left the room in a swirl of liquorice and smoke. After she was gone, Rob wished that he had told her about the tiger. He felt a sudden desperate need to tell somebody—somebody who wouldn't doubt him. Somebody who was capable of believing in tigers.

Chapters Eleven & Twelve

1. B   Rob sighed. "Because Beauchamp, the man who owns it, he had a horse once, called Kentucky Star.

2. D   He took a breath. He opened his mouth and let the words fall out. "I know where there's a tiger." Sistine stood in the drizzly rain and stared at him, her eyes black and fierce. She didn't say "A real one?" She didn't say "Are you crazy?" She didn't say "You're a

big old liar." She said one word: *"Where?"*

3. C And Rob knew then that he had picked the right person to tell.

4. D "We got to walk through the woods," Rob said. He looked doubtfully at Sistine's bright dress and shiny black shoes. "You can give me some of your clothes to wear," she told him. "I hate this dress, anyway." And so he took her to the motel room, and there Sistine stood and stared at the unmade beds and the tattered recliner.

5. B "Oh," she said, her voice full of wonder, "it's perfect. It's like looking in a little wooden mirror."

6. A He thought for a minute about one of the not-wishes he had buried deepest: a friend. He stared at the star and felt the hope and need and fear course through him in a hot neon arc. He shook his head.

Chapters Thirteen & Fourteen

1. D "This is where my mother grew up," Sistine said, swinging her arms wide as she walked. "Right here in Lister. And she said that she always told herself that if she ever made it out of here, she wasn't going to come back. But now she's back because my father had an affair with his secretary, whose name is Bridgette and who can't type, which is a really bad thing for a secretary not to be able to do."

2. A "Where's your mother?" Sistine demanded suddenly. She stopped walking and stared at him. "Shhh," said Rob. "You got to be quiet." He kept walking. "I do not have to be quiet," Sistine called after him. "I want to know where your mother is." He turned around and looked at her. Her hands were on her hips. Her black eyes were narrowed.

3. D Rob watched her. Because she was wearing his jeans and his shirt, it was like looking into a fun-house mirror. It was like watching himself walk away. He shrugged and bent to scratch his legs. He told himself that he didn't care. He told himself that she was leaving soon, anyway. But when he looked up and saw her getting smaller and smaller, it reminded him of his dream. He remembered Sistine riding into the woods on the back of the tiger. And suddenly, he couldn't bear the thought of watching her disappear again.

4. C The cage was made out of rusted chainlink fence. There was a wooden board that served as a roof and there was a chainlink door that was locked tight with three padlocks.

5. B "It's just like the poem says," Sistine breathed. "What?" said Rob. "That poem. The one that goes, 'Tiger, tiger, burning bright, in the forests of the night.' That poem. It's just like that. He burns bright."

6. A   "We could let him go," said Sistine. "We could set him free." She put her hands on her hips. It was a gesture that Rob had already come to recognize and be wary of.

7. B   Then Rob remembered the name of the feeling that was pushing up inside him, filling him full to overflowing. It was happiness. That was what it was called.

Chapters Fifteen & Sixteen

1. B   "I was going to call my mother," said Sistine. "There's a payphone down in the laundry room," said Rob's father. "In the laundry room?" Sistine repeated, her voice full of disbelief. She put her hands on her hips. "We don't got a phone in the room," Rob said to her softly.

2. C   "Rob," his father said as Sistine marched away swinging her arms, "what's that girl doing in your clothes?" "She had on a dress," Rob said. "It was too pretty to wear out in the woods."

3. A   When his mother was alive, the world had seemed full of light. The Christmas before she died, she had strung the outside of their house in Jacksonville with hundreds of white lights. Every night, the house lit up like a constellation, and they were all inside it together, the three of them.

4. C   "I like looking up at things. So do my mum and dad. That's how they met. They were both looking up at the ceiling in the Sistine Chapel and they weren't watching where they were going and they bumped into each other. That's why I'm named Sistine."

5. D   "Because. My dad says it don't do no good to talk about it. He says she's gone and she ain't coming back. . . ."

6. A   "That's why we moved here from Jacksonville. Because everybody always wanted to talk about her. We move down here to get on with things."

7. B   "Good Lord," said Mrs. Bailey to Sistine. "What have you got on?" "Clothes," said Sistine. "Sissy, you look like a hobo. Get in the car." She tapped her high-heeled foot on the gravel.

Chapters Seventeen & Eighteen

1. B   All night, he had tossed and turned, scratching his legs and thinking about the tiger and what Sistine said, that he had to be set free. He had finally decided to get Willie

May's opinion.

2. A   "When I wasn't but little," said Willie May, "my daddy brought me a bird in a cage. It was a green parakeet bird. That bird was so small, I could hold it right in the palm of my hand."

3. D   "Let him go," she said. "You let him go?" Rob repeated, his heart sinking inside him like a stone. "Couldn't stand seeing him locked up, so I let him go."

4. C   Rob took hold of the sheet and, as it billowed out between them, a memory rose up before him: his father standing out in the yard, holding his gun up to the sky, taking aim at a bird.

5. B   . . . when Beauchamp pulled up in his red jeep and honked the horn. "Hey there," he hollered. Beauchamp was a large man with orange hair and an orange beard and a permanent toothpick in the side of his mouth. The toothpick waggled as he talked, as if it was trying to make a point of its own. "We got you on the payroll now, too?" Beauchamp shouted.

6. D   "I got me a wild animal," said Beauchamp. "I got me a wild animal like you would not believe. Right here on my own property. And I got some plans for him. Big plans. But in the meantime, he needs some taking care of, some daily maintenance. You following me, son?"

7. A   He cranked the engine. It roared to life, and they went tearing around behind the Kentucky Star and into the woods. Beauchamp drove like he was crazy. He gunned for trees and then swerved away from them at the last minute, whooping and hollering the whole time.

Chapters Nineteen & Twenty

1. C   "Wow," said Rob. "You own him?" "That's right," said Beauchamp. "Fellow I know owed me some money. Paid me with a tiger. That's the way real men do business. In tigers. He come complete with the cage." The toothpick in the side of his mouth danced up and down; Beauchamp put a finger up to steady it into silence.

2. D   Rob swallowed hard. "How do I get the meat in the cage?" he asked. Beauchamp dug in his pocket and pulled out a set of keys. "With these," he said. He shook the keys and they gave a sad jingle.

3. C   The tiger leaped forward, and Beauchamp took a quick step backward, stumbling. "That's all there is to it," he said, straightening up. His forehead was shiny with sweat, and his hands were trembling.

138

4. A   On the hair-raising ride back to the Kentucky Star, Rob realized who the tiger's stare reminded him of. It was Sistine. He knew that when he told her he had the keys to the cage, her eyes would glow with the same fierce light.

5. B   Rob was dismayed to see that she was still wearing his shirt and jeans. "Where's your dress?" he blurted.

6. D   "I found a book in the library today and read about big cats. Do you know that panthers live in the woods here? We could set the tiger free, and he could live with them. Come on," she said. She started to run.

7. A   Before Rob could think whether it was right or whether it was wrong, he reached out and put his palm on Sistine's neck. He could feel her pulse, beating in time with the tiger's pacing. He whispered to her the same words his mother had whispered to him. "I got you," he told her. "I got good hold of you."

Chapters Twenty-one & Twenty-two

1. A   "You know what?" she said to Sistine. "I know you. You ain't got to introduce yourself to me. You angry. You got all the anger in the world inside you. I know angry when I meet it. Been angry most of my life."

2. C   "This is it: ain't nobody going to come and rescue you," said Willie May. She opened the car door and sat down behind the wheel. "You got to rescue yourself. You understand what I mean?"

3. D   "I think she's a prophetess," said Sistine. "A what?" Rob said. "A prophetess," said Sistine. "They're painted all over the Sistine ceiling. They're women who God speaks through."

4. C   "Beauchamp," his father repeated, low and dark. "Beauchamp. He don't hardly pay me enough to get by, and now he's giving us his rotten meat. He thinks I ain't man enough to put meat on my own table."

5. B   He went and stood in front of the gun case. He didn't unlock it. He just stood and stared and cracked his knuckles.

6. D   He concentrated on that green. He let it seep through a crack in his suitcase of not-thoughts and fill up his head with color. He wondered if Willie May's Cricket had been the same bright and original green. That's what he thought about as he carved. And so he wasn't surprised, when he stopped and held the wood away from himself, to see a wing and a beak and a tiny eye. It was Cricket, Willie May's Cricket, coming to life under his knife.

1. C   She closed her fingers around the little piece of wood, but she didn't open her eyes. She puffed on her cigarette; the long gray ash on the end of it trembled. "Don't need to look," she said finally. The cigarette ash dropped to the floor. "I know what I got in my hand. It's Cricket."

2. B   "Yes, ma'am," said Rob. He stared down at his legs. "I know a wooden bird ain't the same as having a real one." "It ain't," agreed Willie May. "But it soothes my heart just the same."

3. A   So Rob spent his morning following Willie May from room to room, stripping the dirty sheets from the beds.

4. D   "My mother found out that I was wearing your clothes to school," she said. "She took them away from me. I'm in trouble. I'm not supposed to come out here any more."

5. B   She whirled round and faced him. "I want to get in fights," she said fiercely. "I want to hit them back. Sometimes I hit them first."

6. A   "Oh," said Sistine. And Rob realized then why he liked Sistine so much. He liked her because when she saw something beautiful, the sound of her voice changed. All the words she uttered had an *oof* sound to them, as if she was getting punched in the stomach.

1. D   "All I am is somebody speaking the truth. And the truth is: there ain't nothing you can do for this tiger except to let it be."

2. C   Rob looked at Sistine. "Your daddy ain't coming for you," he said softly, shaking his head, amazed at what he suddenly knew to be the truth.

3. A   As they walked back to the Kentucky Star, Rob thought about what Willie May had said about the tiger rising on up. It reminded him of what she had said about his sadness needing to rise up.

4. C   "I come to tell you about the tiger," he said when he caught up with her. "What about him?" "I'm fixing to let him go," said Rob.

5. B   "He's afraid," said Sistine. "He's afraid of the tiger. That's why he's making you feed him." Rob nodded. That was another truth he had known without knowing it, the same as he had known that Sistine's father was not coming back.

6. A   Rob's heart gave another warning thump. Lord only knew what Sistine would say to Beauchamp. But Sistine, as always, surprised him. She smiled sweetly at Beauchamp.

Chapters Twenty-seven & Twenty-eight

1. D   Rob's heart pounded and fluttered in his chest. "What if he eats us?" he asked. "He won't," said Sistine. "He'll leave us alone out of gratitude. We're his emancipators."

2. B   "Get out of the way," he shouted, and they both jumped back from the door and waited. But the tiger ignored them. He continued to pace back and forth in the cage, oblivious to the open door.

3. D   As they stared, the tiger stepped with grace and delicacy out of the cage. He put his nose up and sniffed. He took one tiny step and then another. Then he stopped and stood still. Sistine clapped her hands, and the tiger turned and looked back at them both, his eyes blazing. And then he started to run.

4. A   And Rob saw that hitting wasn't going to be enough. So he did something he thought he would never do. He opened his suitcase. And the words sprang out of it, coiled and explosive. "I wish it had been you!" he screamed. "I wish it had been you that died! I hate you! You ain't the one I need. I need her! I need her!"

5. B   "I ain't going to cry," Rob said, shutting his eyes, but the tears leaked out of him anyway. Then they came in a rush and he couldn't stop. He cried from somewhere deep inside of himself, from the place where his mother had been, the same place that the tiger had been and was gone from now. Rob looked up and saw his father wiping tears from his own eyes. "All right," said his father, holding Rob tight. "That's all right," he said. "You're okay."

6. D   "I went and got your daddy," Willie May told Rob as she swayed back and forth, rocking Sistine. "I figured out what you was gonna do. And there ain't no telling what that tiger would've done once he got out of that cage. I went and got your daddy, so he could save you."

7. C   "We have to have a funeral for him," Sistine said. "He's a fallen warrior. We have to bury him right."

1. B   "I'll say the poem," said Sistine. She folded her hands in front of her and looked down at the ground. "'Tiger, tiger, burning bright / in the forests of the night,'" she recited.

2. A   She reached into her dress pocket and took out the wooden bird and bent down and laid it on top of the tiger. "That ain't nothing," she said to the tiger, "just a little bird to keep you company."

3. C   As he filled the grave, something danced and flickered on his arm. Rob stared at it, wondering what it was. And then he recognized it. It was the sun. Showing up in time for another funeral.

4. D   That night, his father sang to Rob as he put the medicine on his legs. He sang the song about mining for gold, the one that he used to sing with Rob's mother. When he was done with the medicine and the song, he cleared his throat and said, "Caroline loved that song."

5. C   "I'll tell him I was the one who shot him, but you got to admit to letting him go." "Yes, sir," said Rob again.

6. B   "Yes, sir," said Rob. He didn't mind the thought of going back to school. School was where Sistine would be.

7. D   He thought about Sistine and the tiger he wanted to make for her. He thought about what kind of wood he would use and how big he would make the tiger. He thought about how happy Sistine would be when she saw it.

The Tiger Rising

1판 1쇄   2013년 3월 18일
2판 3쇄   2024년 2월 5일

지은이   Kate DiCamillo
기획   이수영
책임편집   차소향 김보경
콘텐츠제작및감수   롱테일 교육 연구소
저작권   명채린
디자인   김진영
마케팅   두잉글 사업 본부

펴낸이 이수영
펴낸곳 롱테일북스
출판등록 제2015-000191호
주소 04033 서울특별시 마포구 양화로 113, 3층(서교동, 순흥빌딩)
전자메일 help@ltinc.net

ISBN 979-11-91343-87-8   14740